the Tree That Time Built

a celebration of nature, science, and imagination

Selected by
Mary Ann Hoberman
and Linda Winston

SOURCEBOOKS
Jabberwocky
AN IMPRINT OF SOURCEBOOKS

Published by Sourcebooks Jabberwocky, an imprint of Sourcebooks, Inc.

P.O. Box 4410, Naperville, Illinois 60567–4410

(630) 961–3900

Fax: (630) 961–2168

www.jabberwockykids.com

Library of Congress Cataloging-in-Publication data is on file with the publisher.

Source of Production: Bang Printing, Brainerd, Minnesota, USA

Date of production: September 2009

Run Number: 10833

Printed and bound in the United States of America.

BG 10 9 8 7 6 5 4 3 2 1

To our families:

Norman Hoberman
Diane Louie, Perry Hoberman, Chuck Hoberman,
Meg Hoberman and Andrew Moszynski,
Jules, Munro, Dorothy, Kit, and Ian

Claudia Gutwirth, Valerie Gutwirth and Elio Gizzi, David and Becca Gutwirth,
Ruby Rose, Sylvie, Jacob, and Samson

About the Audio CD

This audio CD includes:

- 39 minutes of engaging and enriching poetry on 55 tracks. The Table of Contents shows you the tracks and track numbers, plus each poem with a reading displays the track number on the page.

- 44 poems read by 20 poets and artists. Use the Index at the back to find your favorite poems and poets!

- 18 poets, past and present, reading their own work.

- 42 original poem recordings—you'll only find them here.

We hope you'll listen to the CD while you read the book—or enjoy it all on its own!

Contents

MEDITATIONS OF A TORTOISE

SOME PRIMAL TERMITE

EVERYTHING THAT LIVES WANTS TO FLY

I AM THE FAMILY FACE

Hurt No Living Thing

"As buds give rise by growth to fresh buds . . .
so it has been with the great Tree of Life . . ."

Charles Darwin

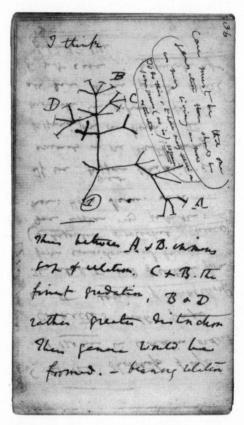

Darwin's Tree of Life diagram,
Notebook B, 1837–1838, p. 36

Introduction

Each of us has a family tree. Some of us have larger families, or more information about our ancestors, than others. But hardly any of us, even those most informed, can trace our families back more than a few centuries; and even then there are always many relatives missing. When you think about how long people have lived on the earth and how long other living things existed here before human beings even appeared, then you realize that our individual family trees are infinitesimal compared with the Tree of Life itself.

The family tree of all life on earth might be called *The Tree That Time Built*. It began putting down its roots millions of years ago. Its branches are crowded with our relatives, both close and distant—far more of them than we might imagine.

Have you ever wondered about why there are so many kinds of living things in the world and where they come from? Or how and why some of them have disappeared? Or how people fit in with all the other forms of life? Scientists and poets alike ask these questions.

Scientists explore these questions through systematic methods and procedures, transforming their observations into ever-unfolding scientific knowledge. Poets, too, through observation and imagination, discover new truths about our world. But in their case they transform their insights into works of art.

Some of those scientists who study life on earth and the connections among living things are called naturalists. In 1831, Charles Darwin, the most prominent naturalist who ever lived, embarked on his famous round-the-world voyage on the HMS *Beagle*. While making detailed studies of plants and animals, he began to discover connections among organisms, recording his observations and reflections in a series of notebooks.

Shortly after he returned home to England in 1837, Darwin sketched a small branching diagram, which he called the Tree of Life. This Tree showed his theory of what we now call evolution, the process by which all species of living beings develop from earlier forms. It depicts the common ancestry of all living things and their changes over time.

Science and art have often been cast as opposites, but the division is an artificial one. Scientists, like poets, depend on imagination for many of their core insights. And poets, like scientists, observe and explore connections within the natural world.

❧ ❧ ❧

In putting this book together, we discovered an interesting parallel between the way naturalists go about things and our own enterprise. It has to do with the matter of collecting. From early boyhood on, Darwin was an avid collector. In his autobiography, he writes: "By the time I went to…day-school my taste for natural history, and more especially for collecting, was well developed. I tried to make out the names of plants, and collected all sorts of things, shells, seals, franks, coins, and minerals. The passion for collecting, which leads a man to be a systematic naturalist…was very strong in me…"

Like Darwin, anthologists are passionate collectors, but the specimens we collect are poems. However, the process of collection in both areas is similar. At first, we simply gathered together as many poems as we could find that fit the subject we had chosen for our book. Then we decided how the book would be organized and we sorted our poems into the various categories we had chosen. The next step was putting the poems into some sort of order within these divisions so that they related thematically to their immediate neighbors. Meanwhile, we continued to find exciting new poems and to discard previously chosen ones; this forced us to rearrange our material constantly.

The poems in this book explore many of the roots and limbs of Darwin's Tree, the branching tree that shows the connections among all forms of life. For some of these poems, we have offered brief comments or pointed out links to other poems.

Try reading the poems slowly. Try reading them aloud. If you like one, read it to a friend. If you're puzzled by one, read it again. You might even memorize a favorite or two. Some of the information in this book may encourage you to look further into a particular aspect of the natural world and, like Darwin, begin some sort of specimen collection. Or possibly this book may inspire you to look for more poems and make your own anthology, including—perhaps— some poems of your own!

Sing of the Earth and sky,
sing of our lovely planet,
sing of the low and high,
of fossils locked in granite.

Sing of the strange, the known,
the secrets that surround us,
sing of the wonders shown,
and wonders still around us.

Aileen Fisher

Oh, Fields of Wonder

Oh, Fields of Wonder

Our sense of wonder seems to be instinctive. From infancy we try to make sense of things by wondering about them. And "wonder," in a happy convergence of meanings, combines in a single word the double sense of both questioning (wondering "about") and marveling (wondering "at").

Both poets and scientists wonder *at* and *about* the world. Out of that wonder, scientists devise experiments to see whether they can verify what they think may be true, while poets craft language to examine and communicate their insights. Sometimes poets even anticipate what scientists later verify, including **evolution** itself. A striking example of this fact occurred within Charles Darwin's family. In an epic poem called "The Temple of Nature," his grandfather, Erasmus Darwin—a doctor, inventor, and poet—foresaw most of what his grandson would later propose as a result of his own investigations.

The poems in the following section speak of the wonderful beginnings of things, from our planet itself adrift in the universe to our own place in space and time. They make connections between pebbles and mountains, people and animals, atoms and stars, while at the same time pondering over the mysterious uniqueness of each living thing.

BIRTH

Oh, fields of wonder

Out of which

Stars are born,

And moon and sun

And me as well,

Like stroke

Of lightning

In the night

Some mark

To make

Some word

To tell.

Langston Hughes

from CIRCLES

Think of a circle   think
our planet
Earth
solid globe
spinning   holding us
holding
oceans and forests and drifting
deserts
in the blackness of space

Think of the sun
our blazing disk   our
daystar
and the planet spinning from
day into night and
return
Think of all that light
washing over us
flowing into starlit dark—
A whirling cycle of days
and nights

Barbara Juster Esbensen

"ATOM FROM ATOM"

Atom from atom yawns as far
As moon from earth, as star from star.

Ralph Waldo Emerson

At the time Emerson wrote this couplet, knowledge about the composition of matter and its atomic structure did not yet exist. Yet here the poet intuits what later scientific studies verified.

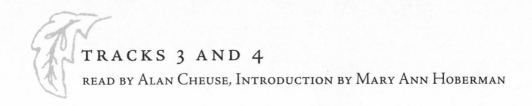

from AUGURIES OF INNOCENCE

To see a World in a grain of sand

And a Heaven in a wild flower,

Hold Infinity in the palm of your hand

And Eternity in an hour.

William Blake

This well-known verse is at once the simplest and most profound expression of a paradoxical truth that continues to engage both poets and scientists. You will find its theme reappearing in poems throughout this collection.

TUNNELS

Under the fields
of grass
are
the tunnels,

the runways
where earthworms
wriggle their
long cool bodies

where sharp-clawed
moles
dig
blindly

where grasshoppers and
beetles
hide their secret
eggs,

the dark winding
tunnels of
a world
under a world.

Lilian Moore

Read this one-sentence poem aloud. In the two syllables of its title and in its first five lines, a single vowel
sound predominates (although its written forms vary), not to return until the final stanza. The poetic
term for this is **assonance**. As you go on reading the poems that follow, be on the lookout for these
recurrences of sounds within poems. Poets often use sound to emphasize meaning.

YOU AND I

Only one I in the whole wide world
And millions and millions of you,
But every you is an I to itself
And I am a you to you, too!

But if I am a you and you are an I
And the opposite also is true,
It makes us both the same somehow
Yet splits us each in two.

It's more and more mysterious,
The more I think it through:
Every you everywhere in the world is an I;
Every I in the world is a you!

Mary Ann Hoberman

THUMBPRINT

In the heel of my thumb
are whorls, whirls, wheels
in a unique design:
mine alone.
What a treasure to own!
My own flesh, my own feelings.
No other, however grand or base,
can ever contain the same.
My signature,
thumbing the pages of my time.
My universe key,
my singularity.
Impress, implant,
I am myself,
of all my atom parts I am the sum.
And out of my blood and my brain
I make my own interior weather,
my own sun and rain.
Imprint my mark upon the world,
whatever I shall become.

Eve Merriam

Consider how this poem moves and develops from its title to its final lines, how "thumbprint" gradually becomes a **metaphor** for a much larger individuality.

THIS WORLD

I would like to write a poem about the world that has in it
  nothing fancy.
But it seems impossible.
Whatever the subject, the morning sun
  glimmers it.
The tulip feels the heat and flaps its petals open
  and becomes a star.
The ants bore into the peony bud and there is a dark
  pinprick well of sweetness.
As for the stones on the beach, forget it.
Each one could be set in gold.
So I tried with my eyes shut, but of course the birds
  were singing.

And the aspen trees were shaking the sweetest music
   out of their leaves.
And that was followed by, guess what, a momentous and
   beautiful silence
   as comes to all of us, in little earfuls, if we're not too
   hurried to hear it.
As for spiders, how the dew hangs in their webs
   even if they say nothing, or seem to say nothing.
So fancy is the world, who knows, maybe they sing.
So fancy is the world, who knows, maybe the stars sing too,
   and the ants, and the peonies, and the warm stones,
   so happy to be where they are, on the beach, instead of being
   locked up in gold.

                                                        Mary Oliver

Here, the poet's desire to write a plain poem about the world—a poem without frills—is defeated by the world itself. Consider the various meanings of "fancy." What are your own associations with the word?

from MARCH '79

Being tired of people who come with words, but no speech,

I made my way to the snow-covered island.

The wild does not have words.

The pages free of handwriting stretched out on all sides!

I came upon the tracks of reindeer in the snow.

Speech but no words.

Tomas Tranströmer

Translated from the Swedish by Robert Bly

In Shakespeare's comedy *As You Like It*, the banished Duke, living contentedly in the forest, says something akin to the thought expressed in this poem: "And this, our life, exempt from public haunt, finds tongues in trees, books in the running brooks, sermons in stones, and good in everything." For a naturalist, too, the deer's hoof marks speak.

from MARCH '79

Sick of those who come with words, words but no language,
I make my way to the snow-covered island.

Wilderness has no words. The unwritten pages
stretch out in all directions.

I come across this line of deer-slots in the snow: a language,
language without words.

Tomas Tranströmer
Translated by Robin Robertson

from MARCH '79

Tired of all who come with words, words but no language
I went to the snow-covered island.
The wild does not have words.
The unwritten pages spread themselves out in all directions!
I come across the marks of roe-deer's hooves in the snow.

Language but no words.

Tomas Tranströmer
Translated by John F. Deane

Here are two more translations of the previous poem by two other translators. Compare the three versions and notice where and how they differ. Do you prefer one of them? The translation of poetry is as much an art as a science, and the translator's choices in moving a poem from one language into another must be both rigorous and imaginative.

IF THEY SPOKE

The animals will never know;
Could not find out; would scarcely care
That all their names are in our books,
And all their images drawn bare.

What names? They have not heard the sound,
Nor in their silence thought the thing.
They are not notified they live;
Nor ask who set them wandering.

Simply they are. And so with us;
And they would say it if they spoke;
And we might listen; and the world
Be uncreated at one stroke.

Mark Van Doren

In one of his most famous sonnets, the poet William Wordsworth wrote: "The world is too much with us late and soon." He used "world" as a metaphor, in which "world" stood for the elaborate and artificial civilization human beings have created that takes them far from their natural origins. In this poem, the poet uses the word in a similar way.

The Sea Is Our Mother

The Sea Is Our Mother

No one knows exactly where or when or how life began on Earth. Maybe in a warm sea or a mud puddle, in the depths of the ocean or underground. Alternatively, some geologists claim that an asteroid might have carried life to our planet.

All living things on Earth are the descendants of simple, single-celled **organisms** that lived more than three and a half billion years ago. Six hundred million years ago, the first simple animals were living in the oceans. They were tiny plantlike worms and jellyfish, floating just above the seafloor.

By 520 million years ago, many new kinds of animals—some hard-shelled—lived in the water. Fifty million years later, armored fish, the first animals with backbones, appeared. Then, fifty million years after that, shellfish, nautiluses, and corals came into existence.

Scientists have already described more than one and a half million **species** of living animals on our planet and many more are yet to be discovered. Most of them live on land, but the ocean contains more of the main divisions, or **phyla**, of the animal kingdom. The ocean's legacy is apparent in our own bodies, which are 70 percent water, most of it salty like the sea itself.

The poems in this section recall life's watery origins as well as the Earth's own geological beginnings. They speak about the planet's ongoing transformations, the diverse creatures engendered in the sea, and about our own human connection to them both.

In *The Voyage of the Beagle*, Darwin wrote of finding deposits of marine fossils high in the Andes Mountains of Chile and Argentina, seven hundred miles inland. His discovery proved that even the most mountainous areas of the earth were once underneath the sea.

THE SEA IS OUR MOTHER

The sea is our mother
    rocking,
      rocking.
See how she fills
    her blue arms
      with gifts—
        with slippery bits,
weed,
  white
    shells,
      fish
as bright as
  wisps
    of moon.
Hear how her voice
  lifts,
    falls,
      lifts
while she sings our
        life.

Tony Johnston

THE VOICE

A sound is slanting on the hills.
It spills through tree and weed and bush.
It pools in mountains tall and green
And still. It is the water's voice.
An ancient voice, an urgent voice
As old as dark, as old as dawn,
It lifts and calls the tortoise forth.
Its coolness whispers *Come. Oh, come.*

The tortoise hears inside its old
Head, the water beckoning,
Unerring knows the path to climb.
It needs no other reckoning.
A deep-sleep walker, up it plods,
Up to the brimming seeps of rain.
It gulps the gleaming water, then
Lumbers slowly down again.

The slow years ebb, the slow years flow.
The water calls; the tortoise goes.

Tony Johnston

DAYBREAK

On the tidal mud, just before sunset,

dozens of starfishes

were creeping. It was

as though the mud were a sky

and enormous, imperfect stars

moved across it slowly

as the actual stars cross heaven.

All at once they stopped,

and as if they had simply

increased their receptivity

to gravity they sank down

into the mud; they faded down

into it and lay still; and by the time

pink of sunset broke across them

they were as invisible

as the true stars at daybreak.

Galway Kinnell

Here the poet has used the same word both to start and to end his poem. By emphasizing the word in this way, he makes it fresh again, reminding us that the "break" of day is that moment when the light of the sun sends the other stars into oblivion. But they are still there.

STARFISH

Spined
With sparks,
Limbed
With flames,

Climbing
The dark
To cling
And shine

Until the
Slow tide
Turns
Again:

Not ever
Knowing
What stars
Are,

But
Even so,
The
Same.

Valerie Worth

Like the previous poem, this one compares starfish with the stars that gave them their name, but here the poet moves beyond metaphor to claim that the two—stars and starfish—are the same. How can this be true?

RIVER INCIDENT

A shell arched under my toes,
Stirred up a whirl of silt
That riffled around my knees.
Whatever I owed to time
Slowed in my human form;
Sea water stood in my veins,
The elements I kept warm
Crumbled and flowed away,
And I knew I had been there before,
In that cold, granitic slime,
In the dark, in the rolling water.

Theodore Roethke

Like the preceding poem, this one speaks of a relationship between two widely separated entities. But here the poet is the descendant of some unknown ancestor lost in the depths of time.

THE JELLYFISH AND THE CLAM

Said the clam to the pink jellyfish,
"You're no more than a lump of wet squish!
You've no backbone or brain,
You're too dull to explain,
When they look at you, people go 'Ish!'"

Said the jellyfish back to the clam,
"I may look like thin raspberry jam,
But you're just a thick shell
And you don't even jell,
So I'm happy to be what I am!"

Well, I say let's give three big cheers
For these two and their lengthy careers.
Though they both may be dull,
With no spine and no skull,
Still they've lasted a half-billion years!

Jeff Moss

SNAIL

Snail upon the wall,
Have you got at all
Anything to tell
About your shell?

Only this, my child—
When the wind is wild,
Or when the sun is hot,
It's all I've got.

John Drinkwater

Intrigued by variation in the patterns and colors of snail shells, Darwin speculated about their possible **adaptive** function. Today evolutionary biologists and geneticists continue to extend this area of research.

FOR RENT: ONE MOON SNAIL SHELL

FOR RENT beside the ocean's shore:
One cozy, well kept
Moon Snail shell.
No snail resides there
Anymore.
(It left and didn't close the door.)

A homeless hermit crab came by.
The shell FOR RENT sign
caught his eye.
He gave the Moon Snail shell a try.

He folded in, umbrella style
and said, "I'll stay in here awhile."

You see, a turtle comes with shell,
a moon snail builds one very well,
but hermit crab lives by his wits
and has to *find* a shell that fits!

Constance Levy

from ROCK

There is stone in me that knows stone,

Substance of rock that remembers the unending unending

Simplicity of rest

While scorching suns and ice ages

Pass over rock-face swiftly as days.

In the longest time of all come the rock's changes,

Slowest of all rhythms, the pulsations

That raise from the planet's core the mountain ranges

And weather them down to sand on the sea-floor.

Kathleen Raine

Geologists who study the history and structure of the Earth deal in millions and billions of years. They call this "deep time." Identifying herself with stone, the poet helps us to grasp the unimaginable slowness of time and its work.

HEIGHT

There was a hill once wanted
to become a mountain
    and
forces underground helped it
    lift itself
    into broad view
and noticeable height:

but the green hills around and even
some passable mountains,
    diminished by white,
wanted it down
so the mountain, alone, found
    grandeur taxing and
    turned and turned
to try to be concealed:

oh but after the rock is
massive and high…!
        how many centuries of rain and
ice, avalanche
and shedding shale
    before the dull mound
can yield to grass!

A. R. Ammons

There is something delightful about attributing human agency to a hill! Haven't we all at some time wanted to be higher and grander than our fellows and then decided that perhaps small is more comfortable after all?

ROCKS

Big rocks into pebbles,

Pebbles into sand.

I really hold a million million rocks here in my hand.

Florence Parry Heide

William Blake's quatrain, quoted earlier, begins: "To see a World in a grain of sand." In this verse, another poet contemplates a handful of sand and arrives at another insight.

DUNES

Taking root in windy sand
   is not an easy
way
to go about
   finding a place to stay.

A ditchbank or wood's-edge
   has firmer ground.

In a loose world though
   something can be started—
a root touch water,
   a tip break sand—

Mounds from that can rise
   on held mounds,
a gesture of building, keeping
   a trapping
into shape.

Firm ground is not available ground.

A. R. Ammons

The final line of this poem, set off by itself, comes as a complete surprise. By rereading the poem with this line in mind, you can see that the poet has been preparing the way for the ending from the very beginning, contrasting soft and hard, loose and firm. And in the poet's careful choice of words, the sounds of the words emphasize the poem's meaning.

Prehistoric Praise

Prehistoric Praise

What exactly are **fossils**? Found in the strata of the earth, fossils are the preserved remains of plants or animals from ages past, long before written records. Animal and plant remains will disintegrate and disappear unless environmental conditions are favorable to their preservation. Today scientists called **paleontologists** (from the Greek: *paleo* = ancient; *onto* = existing things; *ology* = the study of) continue to search for fossils all over the world.

During his visit to Patagonia, Darwin collected a large number of fossils with which he was unfamiliar, thinking they might prove interesting to more experienced naturalists back in England. The captain of the *Beagle* couldn't understand why Darwin was loading up the ship with "useless junk." But the collection turned out to include, among many important finds, the remains of giant versions of armadillos, sloths, and llamas, most of which had heretofore been unknown to science.

Darwin noticed that smaller versions of the gigantic creatures he had discovered were still alive in the same areas where the giant fossils were found. "This wonderful relationship in the same continent between the dead and the living," Darwin wrote, "will…throw more light on the appearance of organic beings on our earth, and their disappearance from it, than any other class of fact."

PREHISTORIC PRAISE

Dinosaurs get all the press
In books and movies
   on subway walls
      long-necked sauropods
      horn-headed triceratops
      sail-backs
         duck-bills
      and, yes indeed, terror-toothed Tyrannosaurus rex reign
Their big bones fill museum halls
Thrashing tail to gaping jaw
   they always inspire awe

But before

      way before reptiles ruled

      other creatures were here:

            sea scorpions the size of automobiles

            dragonflies the size of kites

            fish that climbed to shore

                on finny feet

            trilobites with twenty thousand eyes

            ancestral sharks and gliding rays

They left their shells

      their shape

      their ambition

   on the Earth

They too have worth

   They also amaze

Marilyn Singer

FOSSILS

Older than
books,
than scrolls,

older
than the first
tales told

or the
first words
spoken

are the stories

in forests that
turned to
stone

in ice walls
that trapped the
mammoth

in the long
bones of
dinosaurs—

the fossil
stories that begin
Once upon a time

Lilian Moore

·

Everyone loves stories that begin, "Once upon a time." Here the familiar phrase ends the poem, inviting us to think about it in a new way.

BIRD FOOTPRINT

The footprint of a bird in sand brought your face.
I said, "What of it?"

And the next lone footprint of a bird in the sand
     brought your face again.
I said, "It is written deeper than sand."

I saw a bird wing fixed forty thousand years in a rock,
     a bird wing bringing your foot, your wrist.

Carl Sandburg

Can a bird's footprint resemble a woman's face? In its simple lines, it might evoke the stylized Cycladic sculptures of ancient Greece or the modern drawings of the artist Modigliani. But as the poet shows, there is a more profound connection between the woman and the fossil bird: they share almost identical arm/leg/wing appendages. The primary difference occurs at the "hand," which in birds is a single large long finger with two stubs. This and other modifications fit the wing for its function of flight.

DINOSAUR BONE

Dinosaur bone
alone, alone,
keeping a secret
old as stone

deep in the mud
asleep in the mud
tell me, tell me,
dinosaur bone.

What was the world
when the seas were new
and ferns unfurled
and strange winds blew?

Were the mountains fire?
Were the rivers ice?
Was it mud and mire?
Was it paradise?

How did it smell,
your earth, your sky?
How did you live?
How did you die?

How long have you lain
alone, alone,
Tell me, tell me,
dinosaur bone.

Alice Schertle

OBITUARY FOR A CLAM

Clam, Marine.
Age, 10 years.

Died 300 million years ago
in underwater landslide.
Native of the Tethys Sea.
Loving mother of 198 clams.
Lived a good life
in the shallow water
off the coast of Pangaea.
Survived by
daughter clams,
son clams,
uncle clams,
aunt clams,
clam, clams, clams…
She is missed dearly,
but is fossilized
in the limestone
of a backyard path
in Memphis, Tennessee.

Lisa Westberg Peters

DINOSAURS

Their feet, planted into tar,
drew them down,
back to the core of birth,
and all they are
is found in earth,
recovered, bone by bone,
rising again, like stone
skeletons, naked, white,
to live again, staring,
head holes glaring,
towering, proud, tall,
in some museum hall.

Myra Cohn Livingston

Although a popular view holds that dinosaur fossils have been found in tar pits, that is not the case. Although many kinds of **extinct** animals and plants dating from the Ice Age have been excavated from the La Brea tar pits in California and more recently from other pits in South America, dinosaurs were extinct long before the tar pits existed.

206

A grown-up human being has
 approximately
Two hundred and six different bones
In his or her body.
Can you imagine, then, how many
 different bones
A huge *Tyrannosaurus rex* would have?

Well, a *Tyrannosaurus rex*
Has approximately
Two
Hundred
And six
Different bones
In his or her body—
Same as us.

Hmmmmm...

Jeff Moss

FOREVER

My father tells me
that when he was a boy
he once crashed a ball
through a neighbor's window.

He does not mean to,
but he lies.

I know that aeons ago
the world was ice
and mud
and fish climbed out of the sea
to reptiles on land
to dinosaurs and mammals;

and I know also
that archeologists have found
remains of ancient times
when men lived in caves
and worshiped weather.

Nonetheless I know
that my father,
a grown man,
coming home at night
with work-lines in his face
and love for me hidden behind
the newspaper in his hand,
has always been so
since the world began.

Eve Merriam

We "know" things in a variety of ways. Sometimes the facts that we have learned intellectually seem at odds with the way we feel, as in this poem.

Think Like
a Tree

Think Like a Tree

We wouldn't be here without plants. Without them, we would have no food. Through photosynthesis, their green pigment, chlorophyll, takes light from the sun and changes it into food—food for the plant and then for us and the animals that we consume. Without edible plants most life on earth would not exist.

But our intimate connection with plants does not stop there. In a truly remarkable interchange, animals breathe in oxygen and exhale carbon dioxide while plants do precisely the opposite. Plants and animals are perfect breathing partners.

Like animals, plants evolved in the sea. Neither could migrate to the land until a protective ozone layer was formed. The earliest land plants probably appeared about five hundred million years ago, but the kinds of plants we know today, with their flowers and insect pollinators, didn't develop until over three hundred million years later.

Darwin was fascinated by plants. Although most people associate him primarily with his study of animal evolution, his work with plants contributed even more to the development of his theory. As a university student the only lectures he attended regularly were those given by the botanist J. S. Henslow; and it was Henslow who later recommended him for a position on the *Beagle*. From the **Galápagos** Islands, located in the Pacific Ocean about six hundred miles west of the coast of Ecuador, Darwin sent Henslow more than two hundred plant specimens, a collection that became the best-documented example of the evolution of species on the islands; and after his return to England, he continued to spend much of his time on botanical research.

THINK LIKE A TREE

Soak up the sun

Affirm life's magic

Be graceful in the wind

Stand tall after a storm

Feel refreshed after it rains

Grow strong without notice

Be prepared for each season

Provide shelter to strangers

Hang tough through a cold spell

Emerge renewed at the first signs of spring

Stay deeply rooted while reaching for the sky

Be still long enough to

hear your own leaves rustling.

Karen I. Shragg

Shape poetry, sometimes referred to as **concrete poetry**, is a poetic form in which the arrangement of the words mimics or enhances the subject of the poem. It is found in Greek poetry as early as the third century B.C. and continues to the present day. Lewis Carroll used it in *Alice's Adventures in Wonderland*, where the mouse's "Tale" is shaped like a tail. Here the placement of the poem's lines suggests the shape of an evergreen tree.

FOR THE FUTURE

Planting trees early in spring,
we make a place for birds to sing
in time to come. How do we know?
They are singing here now.
There is no other guarantee
that singing will ever be.

Wendell Berry

In this short and apparently simple verse, a profound truth is embedded: the interconnectedness of various forms of life. Without trees—with their fruits, berries, and nuts, along with the nesting places they provide—what would happen to the creatures that depend on them for sustenance and shelter?

OLD ELM SPEAKS

It is as I told you, Young Sapling.

It will take
autumns of patience
before you snag
your
first
moon.

Kristine O'Connell George

"BREAK OPEN"

Break open
A cherry tree
And there are no flowers
But the spring breeze
Brings forth myriad blossoms

Ikkyu Sojun

CROSS-PURPOSES

The fickle bee believes it's she
Who profits from the flower;
But as she drinks, the flower thinks
She has bee in her power.

Her nectar is the reason
That she blooms, the bee is sure;
But flower knows her nectar
Is there merely for allure.

And as she leaves, the bee believes
She'll sample someone new;
But flower knows that where bee goes,
Her pollen's going, too.

Mary Ann Hoberman

Like many plants and insects, bumblebees and the flowers they pollinate depend on each other for survival. In describing this phenomenon, Darwin refers to the reciprocal effect of species on each other's evolution. He was the first naturalist to describe how the mouthparts of certain insects were perfectly matched to the structure of the flowers that provided their sustenance. Once, he examined a Madagascar orchid with a tubelike organ for secreting nectar that was almost a foot long. He predicted that a moth would be found with a proboscis long enough to probe this orchid's depths. And sure enough, many years after his death, such a moth was finally discovered!

NOSEGAY

Violets, daffodils,
   roses and thorn
were all in the garden
   before you were born.

Daffodils, violets,
   red and white roses
your grandchildren's children
   will hold to their noses.

Elizabeth Coatsworth

THE DANDELION

O dandelion, rich and haughty,

King of village flowers!

Each day is coronation time,

You have no humble hours.

I like to see you bring a troop

To beat the blue-grass spears,

To scorn the lawn-mower that would be

Like fate's triumphant shears.

Your yellow heads are cut away,

It seems your reign is o'er.

By noon you raise a sea of stars,

More golden than before.

Vachel Lindsay

While the diction of this poem may be dated, its subject matter comes through clearly. The poet celebrates the tenacity, as well as the beauty, of a wildflower often considered a weed because it is so common and invasive. But therein lies its strength!

LOST

Stand still. The trees ahead and bushes beside you
Are not lost. Wherever you are is called Here,
And you must treat it as a powerful stranger,
Must ask permission to know it and be known.
The forest breathes. Listen. It answers,
I have made this place around you,
If you leave it you may come back again, saying Here.
No two trees are the same to Raven.
No two branches are the same to Wren.
If what a tree or a bush does is lost on you,
You are surely lost. Stand still. The forest knows
Where you are. You must let it find you.

David Wagoner

Once again, in this poem, we are in the presence of some sort of reciprocity between human beings and the rest of nature. In the poet's view, if we can accept our place in the natural world, we are never truly lost no matter how unfamiliar our surroundings.

THE OAK TREES ARE DREAMING

It is night
The oak trees are dreaming

In their deep night dream-sleep they mumble

They mumble a windsong of fireflies
They mumble a dreamsong of fireflies

They mumble a windsong of moonfire
They mumble a dreamsong of starfire

The leaves dream: dark dreamsthick dreams
The trunks dream: light dreamsfluttering dreams
The limbs dream: deep dreamstangled dreams
The roots dream: sky dreamssun dreams

It is night
The oak trees are dreaming

Patricia Hubbell

Although the first poem in this section tells you to think like a tree, this one describes what it might feel like to be a tree that is dreaming. The word "dream" is repeated again and again until it becomes an incantation, casting a kind of spell, rather like a dream itself.

BEYOND TIME

I am not concerned at all with the golden age of those pines

Or the white time of a carnation

Or the time of the dust on the highway

Or the time of passing clouds.

Whether I lived an age or an instant loses its importance.

It is enough to glance into the eyes of a sunflower,

To grind up thyme in your hand,

Any scent in the infinitive suffices,

Any of the usually unnoticed things of the earth,

Suddenly perceived in such a way

That their shape with eyelids not quite closed

Denies transience (of water, of clouds, of man).

Mieczysław Jastrun

Translated from the Polish by Czesław Milosz

Our perception of time is relative: it can pass slowly or quickly or even, in a moment of heightened perception, vanish entirely, as it seems to do in this poem. When the poet writes "To grind up thyme," he notes that he is using the "infinitive," a verb form with no reference to a particular tense, and thus "beyond time." (Remember: "thyme" is pronounced "time.") He also reminds us how our sense of smell, the most primitive of our senses, has the power to increase our awareness.

MUSHROOMS

Overnight, very
Whitely, discreetly,
Very quietly

Our toes, our noses
Take hold on the loam,
Acquire the air.

Nobody sees us,
Stops us, betrays us;
The small grains make room.

Soft fists insist on
Heaving the needles,
The leafy bedding,

Even the paving.
Our hammers, our rams,
Earless and eyeless,

Perfectly voiceless,
Widen the crannies,
Shoulder through holes. We

Diet on water,
On crumbs of shadow,
Bland-mannered, asking

Little or nothing.
So many of us!
So many of us!

We are shelves, we are
Tables, we are meek,
We are edible,

Nudgers and shovers
In spite of ourselves.
Our kind multiplies:

We shall by morning
Inherit the earth.
Our foot's in the door.

Sylvia Plath

ALL DAY LONG

Beneath the pine tree where I sat
to hear what I was looking at,

then by the sounding shore to find
some things the tide had left behind,

I thought about the hilltop blown
upon by all the winds I've known.

Why ask for any better song
in all the wide world all day long?

David McCord

NATIVE TREES

Neither my father nor my mother knew

the names of the trees

where I was born

what is that

I asked and my

father and mother did not

hear they did not look where I pointed

surfaces of furniture held

the attention of their fingers

and across the room they could watch

walls they had forgotten

where there were no questions

no voices and no shade

Were there trees

where they were children

where I had not been

I asked

were there trees in those places

where my father and mother were born

and in that time did

my father and mother see them

and when they said yes it meant

they did not remember

What were they I asked what were they

but both my father and my mother

said they never knew

W. S. Merwin

A child's frustration when grown-ups cannot answer his questions is palpable in this poem. Here, in focusing his questions on the names of native trees, the poet is making a particular point: by not knowing the names of trees and only caring about them as furniture—dead trees—his parents are cut off from nature. But what is in store for us if, in growing older ourselves, we lose our connection to the natural world?

REPLY TO THE QUESTION:
"How Can You Become a Poet?"

take the leaf of a tree
trace its exact shape
the outside edges
and inner lines

memorize the way it is fastened to the twig
(and how the twig arches from the branch)
how it springs forth in April
how it is panoplied in July

by late August
crumple it in your hand
so that you smell its end-of-summer sadness

chew its woody stem

listen to its autumn rattle

watch as it atomizes in the November air

then in winter
when there is no leaf left

invent one

Eve Merriam

This poem is an extended metaphor in which the study of a leaf becomes the proxy for the attentiveness and invention required in the writing of a poem. It also offers some excellent advice on how to apprentice as a naturalist.

SPRUCE WOODS

It's so still
today that a
dipping bough means
a squirrel
has gone through

A. R. Ammons

"JUST LIVING"

"Just living is not enough,"
Said the butterfly.
"One must have sunshine, freedom,
And a little flower."

Hans Christian Andersen

Meditations of a Tortoise

Meditations of a Tortoise

The giant tortoise's thick impenetrable shell, along with its longevity, make it a popular symbol of eternal life. In both Iroquois and Hindu legends, the earth is supported on the back of a great turtle. The poems in this section tell of tortoises, turtles, lizards, and their other reptile relatives, as well as frogs and toads and other amphibians—all descendents of some of the earliest creatures on earth.

Both reptiles and amphibians live on every continent except Antarctica, but amphibians, unlike reptiles, are absent from island populations. As Darwin noted, amphibians and their eggs are easily killed by immersion in salt water. By contrast, reptiles, which are often found on remote islands, are much better able to survive extraordinary ocean journeys. But how did the giant tortoises get to the remote Galápagos Islands? New **DNA** evidence reveals that several much smaller tortoises native to the South American mainland rafted or floated to one of the newly formed volcanic islands two to three million years ago. The resulting offspring of these animals colonized the other islands in the Galápagos archipelago.

When Darwin first reached the Galápagos, he was misinformed about the famous giant tortoises, which were said to have been imported by buccaneers. He also incorrectly believed, like other naturalists of his time, that the marine iguanas—the only lizards that swim in the ocean—were imports from South America and therefore not unique to the islands.

These claims proved to be untrue. Both these creatures and hundreds of others were found exclusively on these islands. One day the Vice-Governor of the Galápagos told Darwin that he could tell which island a tortoise was from simply by examining the pattern and shape of its shell. This casual remark started a long slow process in Darwin's mind that eventually led him to some of his greatest insights.

MEDITATIONS

OF A TORTOISE

DOZING UNDER A ROSETREE

NEAR A BEEHIVE

AT NOON

WHILE

A DOG

SCAMPERS ABOUT

AND A CUCKOO CALLS

FROM A

DISTANT WOOD

So far as I can see
There is no one like me.

E. V. Rieu

JOURNAL JOTTINGS OF CHARLES DARWIN

The Galápagos Islands, Ecuador:

Such strange creatures!
Huge tortoises, big enough for me to ride;
marine iguanas, dragons dressed in courting colors;
land iguanas, such mild, torpid monsters;
and birds quite fearless and innocent of danger.
What amazes me most are the tiny finches.
Each island's finches have different beaks!
Here both in space and time,
we seem to be brought near to that great fact:
that mystery of mysteries,
the first appearance of new beings on this earth.

Bobbi Katz

What is a **found poem**? It is a poem made from an existing piece of writing that is taken out of its original context and rearranged upon the page. Newspaper excerpts, street signs, advertisements, anything may suggest itself as material. Words may be added or subtracted or left exactly as they were; the meaning may be altered or left the same. Here, the poet has chosen several passages from Darwin's journal, joined them together, and transformed them into a poem.

THE CHAMELEON

Although it may seem very strange,
The colors on a chameleon change
From mousy browns to leafy greens
And several colors in between.
Its very long and sticky tongue
On unsuspecting bugs is sprung.
It lashes out at rapid rates
On unaware invertebrates,
Then just as quickly will retract
With flabbergasted fly intact,
So bugs beware this risky reptilian—
The clever everchanging chameleon.

Douglas Florian

Camouflage in nature is a device of protection and illusion, used by animals to blend into their environments in order to avoid being seen by predators or prey. The most well-known creature using this method is the chameleon, whose coloring not only allows it to blend into its surroundings but also varies according to light and temperature. Indeed, its name is used as a metaphor for anyone who frequently changes personality or appearance.

THE IGUANAS OF SANTIAGO

Once they roamed
these lava flows

        as I do.

They heard the beat
of waves
that break the rocks,
felt the damp
garua.

       As I do

they loved
cactus blooms.

The iguanas saw
the sun rise
  every day.

Like me, they knew
the white clear

       moon.

Here I stand.
The iguanas

     are

      gone.

Tony Johnston

When Darwin visited the Galápagos island of Santiago, then called King James Island, the land iguanas were so plentiful that he recalled, "…we could not for some time find a spot free from their burrows on which to pitch our single tent." Since then not only the iguanas but also all other animals on Santiago have been entirely wiped out by the introduction of nonnative species, such as pigs, rats, cats, and dogs. The *garua* is a damp sea mist.

EARTHWORMS

Garden soil,

Spaded up,

Gleams with

Gravel-glints,

Mica-sparks, and

Bright wet

Glimpses of

Earthworms

Stirring beneath:

Put on the palm,

Still rough

With crumbs,

They roll and

Glisten in the sun

As fresh

As new rubies

Dug out of

Deepest earth

Valerie Worth

Like the poet, Darwin was fascinated by worms, the subject of the very last book he wrote. While he was mostly interested in how earthworms help in soil formation, he studied their general structure and behavior as well, even getting his children to help with his experiments. To see whether earthworms could hear, for example, he played a tin whistle, a bassoon, and a piano in order to find out if they would react. And guess what he discovered? Worms have no sense of hearing at all.

A NARROW FELLOW IN THE GRASS

A narrow Fellow in the Grass
Occasionally rides—
You may have met Him—did you not
His notice sudden is—

the Grass divides as with a Comb—
A spotted shaft is seen—
And then it closes at your feet
And opens further on—

He likes a Boggy Acre
A Floor too cool for Corn—
Yet when a Boy, and Barefoot—
I more than once at Noon

Have passed, I thought, a Whip lash
Unbraiding in the Sun
When stooping to secure it
It wrinkled, and was gone—

Several of Nature's People
I know, and they know me—
I feel for them a transport
Of cordiality—

But never met this Fellow
Attended, or alone
Without a tighter breathing
And Zero at the Bone—

Emily Dickinson

"Fellow" can be defined in several ways: as a man or a boy; as something or someone belonging to the same group. In this poem, Dickinson's use of the word to refer to a snake *anthropomorphizes* the creature (likens it to humans). At the same time, in contrast to her fellow feeling for other of "Nature's People," Dickinson recoils from the snake in instinctive horror. What is it about this animal that frightens so many of us and often makes it a symbol of all that is most primitive and terrifying?

SNAKE

I saw a young snake glide
Out of a mottled shade
And hang, limp on a stone:
A thin mouth, and a tongue
Stayed, in the still air.

It turned; it drew away;
Its shadow bent in half;
It quickened, and was gone.

I felt my slow blood warm.
I longed to be that thing,
The pure, sensuous form.
And I may be, some time.

Theodore Roethke

In an earlier poem, "River Incident," Roethke imagined himself into some prehistoric sea creature. Here, once again, he envisions a nonhuman identity; but now he speculates that this transformation may occur some time in the future. What kind of contrasts can you draw between this poem and the preceding one by Emily Dickinson?

FRILLED LIZARD

Expansion Collar
Instructions for Operation

When not in use, the collar hangs
in compact folds of skin
conveniently tucked away
beneath the wearer's chin.

Activate the collar by
inflation of the lungs,
full extension of the jaws,
projection of the tongue.

Discourages a predator
two times out of three.
Batteries are not required.

Lifetime guarantee.

Alice Schertle

EARLY WALK

On my early walk
I passed the Frog Prince
dead in a rut of the road

his lordly legs spread out
for a royal leap
plump thighs
a fan of tapering toes

his shapely body
flattened
by a passing wheel

and, in a long and purple flume,
like a worm in the wet sand
his gut forlorn.

Virginia Hamilton Adair

Roadkill. We are so accustomed to seeing small dead animals on streets and highways that we seldom give them more than a passing thought. At the same time, the frog who is a prince in disguise is the motif of many beloved fairy tales. Here, with a touch of irony, the poet sees the frog itself, untransformed, as a prince, and invites us to see him that way as well. A "flume" is a narrow water channel.

"A DISCOVERY!"

A discovery!
On my frog's smooth green belly
there sits no button.

Yokoi Yayu

FROG

Pollywiggle	Wet skin
Pollywog	Cold blood
Tadpole	Squats in
Bullfrog	Mucky mud
Leaps on	Leaps on
Long legs	Long legs
Jug-o-rum	Jug-o-rum
Jelly eggs	Jelly eggs
Sticky tongue	Laid in
Tricks flies	Wet bog…
Spied by	Pollywiggle
Flicker eyes	Pollywog.

Mary Ann Hoberman

Can you imagine a world without frogs? In recent decades, a deadly fungal disease, triggered by global warming, has brought on the extinction of dozens of frog species, along with many other species of amphibians, throughout the world. The permeable skin of amphibians makes them especially sensitive to changes in the environment. Their dramatic disappearance warns us of the often harmful effects of climate change on living things.

RAIN FOREST

In the rain forest, where the ground is a limitless
        sponge
           drinking in cloud after cloud's worth
               of water,
the treetops are ablaze with private ponds
        each no bigger than a flower's cup.
Tadpoles hatch within them
        swimming leisurely
        turning into tiny frogs,
           each one master of its estate
where every petal is a teeming shore
        every pool a boundless lake.

Marilyn Singer

THE TORTOISE IN ETERNITY

Within my house of patterned horn
I sleep in such a bed
As men may keep before they're born
And after they are dead.

Sticks and stones may break their bones,
And words may make them bleed;
There is not one of them who owns
An armour to his need.

Tougher than hide or lozenged bark,
Snow-storm and thunder proof,
And quick with sun, and thick with dark,
Is this my darling roof.

Men's troubled dreams of death and birth
Pulse mother-o'-pearl to black;
I bear the rainbow bubble Earth
Square on my scornful back.

Elinor Wylie

Some Primal Termite

Some Primal Termite

Naturalists define fitness as the ability of a species to reproduce itself in the greatest numbers and to adapt to the widest range of environments. According to this definition, insects are the fittest of all living creatures.

As a boy and later at university, Darwin, like many of his contemporaries, was an enthusiastic collector of insects, particularly beetles. At that time every amateur entomologist (from the Greek: *entomon* = insect) was roaming the English countryside, collecting beetles, butterflies, and bugs. Darwin aimed at amassing the biggest and best collection of rare beetles in the country. Almost every day he and one of his cousins went out on insect expeditions.

In his *Autobiography* he recalls the pleasure he took in this pursuit. "No poet ever felt more delight at seeing his first poem published than I did at seeing in Stephen's *Illustrations of British Insects* the magic words, 'captured by C. Darwin, Esq.'" A few years later, on his voyage to South America, his hobby had turned into a real job and he had discovered his true calling, that of a naturalist.

THE TERMITE

Some primal termite knocked on wood
 And tasted it, and found it good,
And that is why your Cousin May
 Fell through the parlor floor today.

Ogden Nash

LINES ON A SMALL POTATO

Reflect upon the dinosaur,

A giant that exists no more.

Though brawny when he was alive,

He didn't manage to survive,

Whereas the unimpressive flea

Continues healthy as can be:

So do not whimper that you're small—

Be happy that you're here at all.

Margaret Fishback

THE MICROSCOPE

Anton Leeuwenhoek was Dutch.
He sold pincushions, cloth, and such.
The waiting townsfolk fumed and fussed
As Anton's dry goods gathered dust.
He worked, instead of tending store,
At grinding special lenses for
A microscope. Some of the things
He looked at were: mosquitoes' wings,
the hairs of sheep, the legs of lice,
the skin of people, dogs, and mice;
ox eyes, spiders' spinning gear,
fishes' scales, a little smear
of his own blood, and best of all,
the unknown, busy, very small
bugs that swim and bump and hop
inside a simple water drop.

Impossible! Most Dutchmen said.

This Anton's crazy in the head.

We ought to ship him off to Spain.

He says he's seen a housefly's brain.

He says the water that we drink

Is full of bugs. He's mad, we think!

They called him *dumkopf,* which means dope.

That's how we got the microscope.

Maxine Kumin

Contrary to popular belief, the Dutch draper named Anton Leeuwenhoek ("lay-ven-hook") did not invent the microscope: other inventors had built such devices decades before he was born. However, because of his skill and patience, Leeuwenhoek was able to build microscopes that magnified objects over two hundred times, ten times the power of then existing instruments. Among his many recorded observations are some of the first of living bacteria.

THINGS ON A MICROSCOPE SLIDE

Your sore-throat germ may say, "Heh heh,
I'm little! I can hide!"
Till a doctor grabs it by the tail
And slings it on a slide,

A kind of flat glass-bottomed ark
Where he collects, this Noah,
The eyes of flies, the knees of fleas,
The toes of protozoa.

X. J. Kennedy

EVERY INSECT

Every Insect (ant, fly, bee)
Is divided into three:
One head, one chest, one stomach part.

Some have brains.
All have a heart.

Insects have no bones.

No noses.

But with feelers they can smell
Dinner half a mile away.

Can your nose do half as well?

Also you'd be in a fix
With all those legs to manage:
Six.

Dorothy Aldis

This poem imparts useful information in a humorous way. Part of the fun is the way its lines are placed on the page. How else could the poet have arranged them?

97

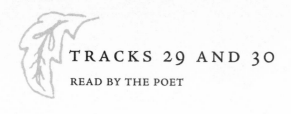

CRICKET

A cricket's ear is in its leg.
A cricket's chirp is in its wing.
A cricket's wing can sing a song.
A cricket's leg can hear it sing.

Imagine if your leg could hear.
Imagine if your ear could walk.
Imagine if your mouth could swing.
Imagine if your arm could talk.

Would everything feel upside down
And inside out and wrongside through?
Imagine how the world would seem
If you became a cricket, too.

Mary Ann Hoberman

Animals make sounds in a variety of ways. Frogs vibrate their air sacs, woodpeckers drum on hard surfaces, flies rapidly beat their wings, and male crickets rub their wings together. Hearing organs also vary both in structure and placement; thus, for example, all crickets, both male and female, have special eardrums located on their front legs just below the knees.

THE SPIDER

With six small diamonds for his eyes
He walks upon the Summer skies,
Drawing from his silken blouse
The lacework of his dwelling house.

He lays his staircase as he goes
Under his eight thoughtful toes
And grows with the concentric flower
Of his shadowless, thin bower.

His back legs are a pair of hands,
They can spindle out the strands
Of a thread that is so small
It stops the sunlight not at all.

He spins himself to threads of dew
Which will harden soon into
Lines that cut like slender knives
Across the insects' airy lives.

He makes no motion but is right,
He spreads out his appetite
Into a network, twist on twist,
This little ancient scientist.

He does not know he is unkind,
He has a jewel for a mind
And logic deadly as dry bone,
This small son of Euclid's own.

Robert P. Tristram Coffin

Euclid of Alexandria was a Greek mathematician whose work, *Elements*, presents the earliest comprehensive and logical system of geometry. Perhaps in acknowledgment, this poem itself uses a completely regular and logical form.

BEES STOPPED

Bees stopped on the rock

and rubbed their headparts and wings

rested then flew on:

ants ran over the whitish greenish reddish

plants that grow flat on rocks

and people never see

because nothing should grow on rocks:

I looked out over the lake

and beyond to the hills and trees

and nothing was moving

so I looked closely

along the lakeside

under the old leaves of rushes

and around clumps of drygrass

and life was everywhere

so I went on sometimes whistling

A. R. Ammons

How many things do we not notice simply because of our preconceptions? The plants growing on rocks in this poem are called "lichen"; but rather than using their name, the poet describes them, thus compelling us to visualize them in our mind's eye.

"THE PEDIGREE OF HONEY"

The Pedigree of Honey
Does not concern the Bee—
A Clover, any time, to him,
Is Aristocracy—

Emily Dickinson

"METAMORPHOSIS"

Metamorphosis:
Caterpillar, chrysalis,
Butterfly is born.

Mary Ann Hoberman

The type of poem known as a haiku calls for three lines of five, seven, and five syllables. I was delighted when I discovered that the words that define and mark the stages of a butterfly's development slipped so perfectly—rhythmically, melodically, and visually—into the haiku form.

COCOON

The little caterpillar creeps
Awhile before in silk it sleeps.
It sleeps awhile before it flies,
And flies awhile before it dies,
And that's the end of three good tries.

David McCord

BUTTERFLY

Butterfly, the wind blows sea-ward, strong beyond the garden wall!
Butterfly, why do you settle on my shoe, and sip the dirt on my shoe,
Lifting your veined wings, lifting them? big white butterfly!

Already it is October, and the wind blows strong to the sea
from the hills where snow must have fallen, the wind is polished with snow.
Here in the garden, with red geraniums, it is warm, it is warm
but the wind blows strong to sea-ward, white butterfly, content on my shoe!

Will you go, will you go from my warm house?
Will you climb on your big soft wings, black-dotted
as up an invisible rainbow, an arch
till the wind slides you sheer from the arch-crest
and in a strange level fluttering you go out to sea-ward, white speck!

Farewell, farewell, lost soul!
you have melted in the crystalline distance,
it is enough! I saw you vanish into air.

D. H. Lawrence

The butterfly described here is probably *Pieris brassicae*, the Large Cabbage White, which is the largest white butterfly in England and on the Continent. It does not inhabit the Americas. Its poisonous larvae, brightly colored to warn off predators, feed on members of the cabbage family. It is a strong flyer and often migrates throughout Europe and the British Isles.

SEEN FROM ABOVE

On a dirt road lies a dead beetle.
Three little pairs of legs carefully folded on his belly.
Instead of death's chaos—neatness and order.
The horror of this sight is mitigated,
the range strictly local, from witchgrass to spearmint.
Sadness is not contagious.
The sky is blue.

For our peace of mind, their death seemingly shallower,
animals do not pass away, but simply die,
losing—it seems to us—a stage less tragic.
Their humble little souls do not haunt our dreams,
they keep their distance,
know their place.

So here lies the dead beetle on the road,

glistens unlamented when the sun hits.

A glance at him is as good as a thought:

he looks as if nothing important had befallen him.

What's important is valid supposedly for us.

For just our life, for just our death,

a death that enjoys an extorted primacy.

Wisława Szymborska

Translated from the Polish by Magnus J. Krynski

and Robert A. Maguire

At first this poem's title seems merely descriptive: the poet is looking down at a dead beetle on the road. But by the end of the poem, "Seen From Above" has taken on an extended and more challenging meaning.

LOCUST

One locust alone doesn't make any trouble.

The same thing is true when the locusts are double.

Three locusts are lovely.

Four locusts are sweet.

Five locusts collected do not overeat.

Six locusts, one locus, cause little complaint,

While seven assembled show equal restraint.

Eight locusts located together are fine.

It's equally fine when their number is nine.

Ten locusts dine lightly wherever they dine.

A dozen?

A hundred?

A thousand?

It's strange;

But when they feel crowded, they totally change.

Ten thousand?

A million?

The figure grows bigger;

But how many locusts are needed to trigger

That change in complexion, behavior, and mood

That changes the way that they feel about food?

One locust alone simply nibbles and stops;

But locusts in crowds chew up all of the crops.

Mary Ann Hoberman

For centuries people have wondered about the "tipping point" of a swarm of locusts, the number required to turn a haphazard group of individual insects, each foraging on its own, into a disciplined army, moving in the same direction and devouring everything in its path. Recently a group of scientists in Australia conducted an experiment to try to discover this transformative number and came up with thirty. It was with this number that the locusts formed a line and began moving in unison. The scientists speculated that the reason for this behavior was that, while there is safety in numbers, a group of this size becomes conspicuous to predators and therefore must start moving, both to find food and to avoid becoming food itself. But when I wrote this poem, this research had not yet been done.

FLIES

Flies wear
Their bones
On the outside.

Some show dead
Gray, as bones
Should seem,

But others gleam
Dark blue, or bright
Metal-green,

Or a polished
Copper, mirroring
The sun:

If all bones
Shone so, I
Wouldn't mind

Going around
In my own
Skeleton.

Valerie Worth

THE WALKINGSTICK

The walkingstick is thin, not thick,
And has a disappearing trick:
By looking like a twig or stalk,
It lives another day to walk.

Douglas Florian

Here is another example of camouflage, that of the stick insects. They are notable for their variety, with different species able to mimic sticks, twigs, leaves, and stems. This mimicry even extends to their eggs, which often resemble plant seeds.

ANTS ON THE MELON

Once when our blacktop city
was still a topsoil town
we carried to Formicopolis
a cantaloupe rind to share
and stooped to plop it down
in their populous Times Square
at the subway of the ants

and saw that hemisphere
blacken and rise and dance
with antmen out of hand
wild for their melon toddies
just like our world next year
no place to step or stand
except on bodies.

Virginia Hamilton Adair

Ants belong to the **family** Formicidae and "polis" comes from the Greek word for "city"—hence the tongue-in-cheek word for ant city coined in the poem. Ants are social insects whose organized colonies do indeed resemble cities. Scientists have noted their division of labor whereby various groups carry out specialized tasks on behalf of the community as a whole rather than for any individual benefit. Evolutionary biologists use the term **altruism** in a specialized sense to refer to this behavior. But while the portrait of a jolly scene of insect inebriation brings a smile during most of this poem, the last line is as sobering as a splash of cold water.

FLY, DRAGONFLY!

Water nymph, you have
climbed from the shallows to don
your dragon-colors.

Perched on a reed stem
all night, shedding skin, you dry
your wings in moonlight.

Night melts into day.
Swift birds wait to snap you up.
Fly, dragonfly! Fly!

Joyce Sidman

Everything That Lives Wants to Fly

Everything That Lives Wants to Fly

Both awe and envy of fellow creatures possessing the gift of flight seem to be deeply embedded in the human psyche. In the continuing scientific debate about the origin and evolution of birds, some scientists espouse the idea that birds descend from tree-dwelling gliders (the "trees-down" hypothesis). Other scientists argue that flight occurred in birds that originally ran quickly along the ground (the "ground-up" hypothesis). Still others propose that early birds might have been at home both in the trees and on the ground, like modern crows. The earliest known bird, *Archaeopteryx* (from ancient Greek: *archaeo* = ancient; *pteryx* = feather or wing), lived about 150 million years ago.

Along with *Archaeopteryx*, Darwin's finches play a key role in evolutionary theory. During his voyage to the Galápagos, Darwin collected a group of bird specimens with differently shaped beaks. Not being a bird expert, he was unaware of the significance of what he had found—he thought he had a mix of blackbirds, "gross beaks," and finches—and did not bother to record each bird's island of origin.

It was only after Darwin had returned to England with his preserved bird specimens that his colleague, John Gould, an eminent ornithologist, recognized that *all* the birds were ground finches and together formed an entirely new group, containing twelve different species. Gould told Darwin that these finches were related to other species from South America.

Darwin pondered over this information. He speculated that a storm might have blown a flock of finches from the mainland over to the Galápagos, where they had landed on various islands. On each of these islands, the birds would have found different kinds of seeds and insects to eat. Darwin hypothesized that over the course of many generations the different beaks in each group of finches had evolved, by means of **natural selection**, as **adaptations** best fitted to the kinds of foods available in the specific environments of the different islands. This breakthrough insight provided significant support for his evolutionary theory.

FEATHERS

Everything that lives
wants to fly,
a Mohawk friend
said to me
one winter afternoon
as we watched
grosbeaks take seeds,
fluttering close
to our eyes.

Those were
dinosaurs once,
he said,
but they
made a bargain.
They gave up
that power
in return for
the Sky.

Joseph Bruchac

While scientists continue to investigate and debate the origins of birds, the widely held belief that they are descendants of "flying dinosaurs" is expressed in this poem.

GALAPAGOS RAIL

The tiny rail is loath to fly.
It sticks close to the ground
and seeks out insects. It is shy.
The tiny rail is loath to fly.
For succulent arachnidae,
it probes the leafy mounds.
The tiny rail is loath to fly.
It sticks close to the ground.

Tony Johnston

The rail is a small, secretive wetland bird. Why would it be "loath to fly"? Adaptation holds the key. Descended from land birds, which had to be strong fliers to journey to the Galápagos from places of origin six hundred miles away, these island rails, with no predators to threaten them, had no reason to leave the ground and so eventually lost the power of flight. ("Arachnidae" are members of a large class of animals, which includes spiders, scorpions, and mites. Unlike insects, they have four pairs of legs.)

THE DIPPERS

Through splash and spray
Of waterfalls
Skip the little dippers.
I think that they
Would gladly trade
Their oily wings for flippers.
Inside a stream
They swim supreme,
For minutes if they wish—
These funny little songbirds
Who think that they are fish.

Douglas Florian

Here is another example of adaptation in birds. Dippers live in river habitats, but resemble terrestrial birds more than water ones. However, as the poem tells us, their wings can be used as flippers underwater. Other adaptations include underwater vision, nasal flaps, and a special gland secreting oil that allows them to waterproof their feathers.

THE SEED EATERS

The seed eaters, the vegetarian birds,
Redpolls, grosbeaks, crossbills, finches, siskins,
Fly south to winter in our north, so making
A sort of Florida of our best blizzards.

Weed seeds and seeds of pine cones are their pillage.
Alder and birch catkins, such vegetable
Odds and ends as the winged keys of maple
As well as roadside sumac, red-plush-seeded.

Hi! With a bounce in snowflake flocks come juncos
As if a hand had flipped them and tree sparrows,
Now nip and tuck and playing tag, now squatting
All weather-proofed and feather-puffed on snow.

Hard fare, full feast, I'll say, deep cold, high spirits.
Here's Christmas to Candlemas on a bunting's budget.
From this old seed eater with his beans, his soybeans,
Cracked corn, cracked wheat, peanuts and split peas, hail!

Robert Francis

Candlemas, a Christian holiday, evolved out of an ancient celebration of the first day of spring. Today it occurs on the same date as Groundhog Day, February 2. On this day, as tradition has it, if the groundhog sees its shadow upon emerging from its den, there will be six more weeks of winter. Or in the words of an old English proverb: "If Candlemas Day be bright and clear / there'll be two winters in the year."

A LIVING

A bird
picks up its seeds or little snails
between heedless earth and heaven
in heedlessness.

But, the plucky little sport, it gives to life
song, and chirruping, gay feathers, fluff-shadowed warmth
and all the unspeakable charm of birds hopping and fluttering
     and being birds,
       —And we, we get it all from them for nothing.

D. H. Lawrence

OCTOBER TEXTURES

The brushy and hairy,
tassely and slippery

willow, phragmite,
cattail, goldenrod.

The fluttery, whistley
water-dimpling divers,

waders, shovelers,
coots and rocking scaup.

Big blue, little green,
horned grebe, godwit,

bufflehead, ruddy,
marsh hawk, clapper rail.

Striated water
and striated feather.

The breast of the sunset.
The phalarope's breast.

May Swenson

Like many writers for whom English is a second language (she grew up in a Swedish-speaking family in Utah), May Swenson delighted in unfamiliar and unusual words. In this poem she plays with the captivating names of some of the birds and plants that intermingle in the autumn landscape.

SOMETHING TOLD THE WILD GEESE

Something told the wild geese
  It was time to go.
Though the fields lay golden
  Something whispered,—"Snow."
Leaves were green and stirring,
  Berries, luster-glossed,
But beneath warm feathers
  Something cautioned,—"Frost."
All the sagging orchards
  Steamed with amber spice,
But each wild breast stiffened
  At remembered ice.
Something told the wild geese
  It was time to fly,—
Summer sun was on their wings,
  Winter in their cry.

Rachel Field

Animal migration is one of nature's mysteries. How do wild geese know precisely when to migrate and how do they return to the same winter habitat year after year? In the spring how do they find their way home? It is known that they use both the stars and the sun as navigational aids; in addition the winds and the earth's magnetic field may help them. Flying at speeds as high as sixty miles an hour, often covering distances of three thousand miles in a single migratory season, wild geese are among nature's marvels.

HUMMING-BIRD

I can imagine, in some otherworld
Primeval-dumb, far back
In that most awful stillness, that only gasped and hummed,
Humming-birds raced down the avenues.

Before anything had a soul,
While life was a heave of Matter, half inanimate,
This little bit chipped off in brilliance
And went whizzing through the slow, vast, succulent stems.

I believe there were no flowers then,
In the world where the humming-bird flashed ahead of creation.
I believe he pierced the slow vegetable veins with his long beak.

Probably he was big
As mosses, and little lizards, they say, were once big.
Probably he was a jabbing, terrifying monster.

We look at him through the wrong end of the long telescope of Time.
Luckily for us.

D. H. Lawrence

In this poem, Darwin's discovery of giant fossil forms in the Galápagos may have been the inspiration for Lawrence's wildly implausible giant hummingbird, a delightful example of **poetic license**.

PEACOCK DISPLAY

He approaches her, trailing his whole fortune,
Perfectly cocksure, and suddenly spreads
The huge fan of his tail for her amazement.

Each turquoise and purple, black-horned, walleyed quill
Comes quivering forward, an amphitheatric shell
For his most fortunate audience: her alone.

He plumes himself. He shakes his brassily gold
Wings and rump in a dance, lifting his claws
Stiff-legged under the great bulge of his breast.

And she strolls calmly away, pecking and pausing,
Not watching him, astonished to discover
All these seeds spread just for her in the dirt.

David Wagoner

"The sight of a feather in a peacock's tail, whenever I gaze on it, makes me sick!" These are Darwin's own words! But why did the flamboyant tail of the male peacock trouble him so? Simply because such a showy appendage had no apparent utility; indeed, it could actually damage a peacock's struggle for existence by making him more visible to his enemies. This state of affairs hardly fit in with Darwin's theory of **natural selection**. To account for the apparent contradiction, he proposed a theory of **sexual selection**, of which ornamentation is one feature. For example, a more showy male (and in some cases a showy female) may have a reproductive advantage over a less gaudy competitor. However, the matter is far from settled and indeed has raised an abundance of new questions that scientists are still exploring.

THE BAT

By day the bat is cousin to the mouse.
He likes the attic of an aging house.

His fingers make a hat about his head.
His pulse beat is so slow we think him dead.

He loops in crazy figures half the night
Among the trees that face the corner light.

But when he brushes up against a screen,
We are afraid of what our eyes have seen:

For something is amiss or out of place
When mice with wings can wear a human face.

Theodore Roethke

Although bats resemble mice, as the poet notes in this poem, bats are not rodents. Recent evidence indicates that bats may be more closely related to primates (which include humans) than to rodents. And as the only mammals that can fly, they are unique.

I Am the Family Face

I Am the Family Face

Family members tend to resemble each other, whether in physical features or personality traits. Sometimes this can feel oppressive, a denial of our individual uniqueness, a predetermination of who we are and what we may become. It can also be comforting, an evidence of our connection to the past as well as a promise of ongoing continuity. And this continuum extends to our earliest ancestors, without whom we would not be here today. Human beings (Species: *Homo sapiens*) are members of the Hominid Family, which in turn belongs to the Primate Order and the Mammal Class. Darwin knew that any explanation of the evolution of species would have to account for human beings. At first he hesitated to put forth his ideas, but in 1871 he addressed the topic of human origins in a book entitled *The Descent of Man*. In his comparisons of the anatomical similarities between humans and their closest living relatives, the chimpanzees, Darwin found persuasive evidence that both species have descended from a common ancestor. Recent comparisons of the **genomes** of chimps and humans have confirmed Darwin's claim.

In 1872 Darwin published *The Expression of Emotions in Man and Animals*. In this book, he noted that "the young and the old of widely different races, both with man and animals, express the same state of mind by the same movements." He also compared the laughter of humans and monkeys, once again underlining their strong similarities.

HEREDITY

I am the family face;
Flesh perishes, I live on,
Projecting trait and trace
Through time to times anon,
And leaping from place to place
Over oblivion.

The years-heired feature that can
In curve and voice and eye
Despise the human span
Of durance—that is I;
The eternal thing in man,
That heeds no call to die.

Thomas Hardy

ANTHROPOIDS

The next time you go to the zoo
The zoo
Slow down for a minute or two
Or two
    And consider the apes
    All their sizes and shapes
For they all are related to you
To you.

Yes, they all are related to you
To you
And they all are related to me
To me
    To our fathers and mothers
    Our sisters and brothers
And all of the people we see
We see.

The chimpanzees, gorillas, and all
And all
The orangutans climbing the wall
The wall
    These remarkable creatures
    Share most of our features
And the difference between us is small
Quite small.

So the next time you go to the zoo
The zoo
Slow down for a minute or two
Or two
    And consider the apes
    All their sizes and shapes
For they all are related to you
To you.

Mary Ann Hoberman

One day several years ago when the editors of this book were talking together about poetry and how some poems beget others, Mary Ann Hoberman mentioned that one of her own poems was inspired by the rhythm and **cadence** of a Rudyard Kipling poem from his *Just So Stories*. She then recited "Anthropoids." This prompted Linda Winston to suggest that they put together a collection of poems expanding upon the poem's theme. And so this anthology was born!

"Anthropoid" means "manlike" and is the name of the ape family that most closely resembles man. **Genetically**, chimpanzees and human beings are more than 96 percent identical and evolved separately from a common ancestor that lived about 6 million years ago.

THE PANTHER

His vision, from the constantly passing bars,
has grown so weary that it cannot hold
anything else. It seems to him there are
a thousand bars and behind the bars, no world.

As he paces in cramped circles, over and over,
the movement of his powerful soft strides
is like a ritual dance around a center
in which a mighty will stands paralyzed.

Only at times, the curtain of the pupils
lifts quietly—. An image enters in,
rushes down through the tensed, arrested muscles,
plunges into the heart and is gone.

Rainer Maria Rilke
Translated from the German by Stephen Mitchell

Private collections of wild animals held in captivity date back to ancient times. The first collections open to the public (called zoos, short for zoological gardens) originated in the nineteenth century. While many zoos today exhibit animals in environments that replicate their native habitats, traditional zoos have kept animals captive in narrow cages. In this poem, written almost a century ago, the poet observes a powerful jungle animal confined to a cage in the Paris zoo.

THE DANCING BEAR

Slowly he turns himself round and round,
　Lifting his paws with care,
Twisting his head in a sort of bow
　To the people watching there.

His keeper, grinding a wheezy tune,
　Jerks at the iron chain,
And the dusty, patient bear goes through
　His solemn tricks again.

Only his eyes are still and fixed
　In a wide, bewildered stare,
More like a child's lost in woods at night
　Than the eyes of a big brown bear.

Rachel Field

Like the previous poem, this one looks at a fellow creature in captivity and empathizes deeply with him.
Here he is seen as a lost child. There is irony in the comparison, since the very place a bear would not
feel lost is in the woods. An earlier poem comes to mind, "Lost," by David Wagoner, where the poet
instructs us on how to find ourselves in the forest.

THE POLAR BEAR

The polar bear by being white
gives up his camouflage at night.
And yet, without a thought or care,
he wanders here, meanders there,
and gaily treads the icy floes
completely unconcerned with foes.
For after dark nobody dares
to set out after polar bears.

Jack Prelutsky

Why is a polar bear white? Contrary to popular belief, it probably is not for reasons of camouflage, since the polar bear is not threatened by any natural enemies. Rather, its white fur defends it against the Arctic cold. Its "white" hairs are actually transparent and hollow, and act as solar collectors transmitting heat from the sun. We see them as white, as we do the snow and the ice, due to the reflection of the sunlight.

from SONG OF MYSELF

I think I could turn and live with animals, they are so placid
    and self-contained,
I stand and look at them long and long.
They do not sweat and whine about their condition,
They do not lie awake in the dark and weep for their sins,
They do not make me sick discussing their duty to God,
Not one is dissatisfied, not one is demented with the mania of
    owning things,
Not one kneels to another, nor to his kind that lived thousands
    of years ago,
Not one is respectable or unhappy over the whole earth…

Walt Whitman

The first edition of *Leaves of Grass* by Walt Whitman was published anonymously in 1855 and consisted of twelve poems, of which "Song of Myself" is the first. By the time he died in 1892, his book had gone through nine editions and contained almost four hundred poems. In this work, Whitman takes on the persona of the common man or of America itself. He is often regarded as the first truly American poet; both his style and his subject matter were unique.

IN PRAISE OF SELF-DEPRECATION

The buzzard has nothing to fault himself with.
Scruples are alien to the black panther.
Piranhas do not doubt the rightness of their actions.
The rattlesnake approves of himself without reservations.

The self-critical jackal does not exist.
The locust, alligator, trichina, horsefly
live as they live and are glad of it.

The killer-whale's heart weighs one-hundred kilos
but in other respects it is light.

There is nothing more animal-like
than a clear conscience
on the third planet of the Sun.

Wisława Szymborska
Translated from the Polish by Magnus J. Krynski and Robert A. Maguire

In another translation, this poem is titled "In Praise of Feeling Bad About Yourself." It is tempting to idealize the behavior of nonhuman animals, contrasting their instinctive conduct with our own failings—as Whitman does in "Song of Myself"—while forgetting Alfred Tennyson's conflicting description of "Nature, red in tooth and claw." It comes as quite a surprise when the tables are turned, as in this witty poem.

PROCYONIDAE

If you give a little whistle,

You might meet a cacomistle,

A coati or olingo

Or a raccoon with a ring-o;

I can name them by the dozens

And all of them are cousins

      And they're all related to the giant panda!

The kinkajou's another

That is practically a brother

To coatis and olingos

And to raccoons with their ring-os;

And every single one of them

Is different, that's the fun of them

      Yet every one's related to the panda!

Now they all have different faces

And they live in different places

And they all have different sizes,

Different noses, different eyeses;

But the family name for all of them

Is just the same for all of them

And each one is related to the panda!

Mary Ann Hoberman

When I wrote this poem, the giant panda was classified as a member of the Procyonidae (raccoon) family; and I had great fun connecting the beloved creature to its curiously named relatives. However, in the late 1980s, scientists using DNA studies relocated the giant panda into the Ursidae (bear) family. We include this poem, with its misinformation, to illustrate the self-correcting nature of scientific classification in the light of new information and new methods of inquiry. The giant panda has become a symbol for endangered species. Despite great efforts to save its habitat and protect it from poachers, its future remains uncertain.

SHEEP

From where I stand the sheep stand still
As stones against the stony hill.

The stones are gray
And so are they.

And both are weatherworn and round,
Leading the eye back to the ground.

Two mingled flocks—
The sheep, the rocks.

And still no sheep stirs from its place
Or lifts its Babylonian face.

Robert Francis

BIRTH OF PHILOSOPHY

The heath sheep glares at me with frightened awe
as though I were the first of men it saw.
Contagious glare! We stand as though asleep;
it seems the first time that I see a sheep.

Christian Morgenstern
Translated from the German by Max Knight

What is philosophy? Its origin is Greek: *philos* = loving; *sophos* = wise; literally, therefore: "love of wisdom." In Homer's *Odyssey*, when the hero Odysseus returns home after his long travels, he is first recognized by his dog, Argos. Writing about this encounter, the naturalist Loren Eiseley said: "One does not meet oneself until one catches [one's] reflection from an eye other than human." In this short poem, the divide between humans and other animals has been bridged, if only for a moment.

THE MASKED SHREW

...the masked shrew...dies of old age after only about
a year of fast-paced gluttonous life.—Life

A penny is heavier than the shrew.

Dim-eyed, and weaker than a worm,

this smallest mammal, cannoned by a sudden noise,

lies down and dies.

No furnace gluttons fiercer than the shrew,

devouring daily with relentless appetite

four times her inchling body's weight.

More extravagant than the humming-bird's, the shrew's

heart beats per minute twice four hundred times.

If foodless for six hours, she is dead.

The helpless, hungry, nervous shrew

lives for a year of hurly-burly

and dies intolerably early.

Isabella Gardner

Life was a popular weekly news magazine throughout the mid-twentieth century, the first to emphasize photography to tell its stories. While it concentrated on politics and culture, it also published pieces on nature and science, one of which inspired this poem.

"LITTLE BY LITTLE"

Little by little, wean yourself.

This is the gist of what I have to say.

From an embryo, whose nourishment comes in the blood,
move to an infant drinking milk,
to a child on solid food,
to a searcher after wisdom,
to a hunter of more invisible game.

Think how it is to have a conversation with an embryo.
You might say, "The world outside is vast and intricate
There are wheatfields and mountain passes, and orchards in bloom.

At night there are millions of galaxies, and in sunlight
the beauty of friends dancing at a wedding."

You ask the embryo why he, or she, stays cooped up
in the dark with eyes closed.
Listen to the answer.

There is no "other world."
I only know what I've experienced.
You must be hallucinating.

Jelaluddin Rumi
Translated from the Persian by Coleman Barks

Rumi was a thirteenth-century Persian mystical poet. In this poem the embryo's response to the question is like a pebble thrown in a pond—the ripples it sets off in your mind keep getting larger. Today **embryology** is at the forefront of new discoveries in evolution.

Hurt No Living Thing

Hurt No Living Thing

It is natural for species to go extinct, but the rate at which this is happening today is unprecedented. A biological event of this magnitude has not happened since the Cretaceous period, one hundred million years ago, when the dinosaurs and most other forms of land and sea animals disappeared. Today, however, it is not cosmic forces but rather our own behavior that is responsible.

Human beings are in process of polluting and exhausting the world's resources. To assure our survival and that of future generations, we must act now to restore and preserve the environment so that Earth will remain rich in life-forms. Only then will Darwin's great Tree of Life continue to grow and flourish. As a Kenyan proverb tells us:

Treat the Earth well.
It was not given to you by your parents.
It was loaned to you by your children.

HURT NO LIVING THING

Hurt no living thing:
   Ladybird, nor butterfly
Nor moth with dusty wing,
   Nor cricket chirping cheerily,
Nor grasshopper so light of leap.
   Nor dancing gnat, or beetle flat,
Nor harmless worms that creep.

Christina Rossetti

LIVING

The fire in leaf and grass
so green it seems
each summer the last summer.

The wind blowing, the leaves
shivering in the sun,
each day the last day.

A red salamander
so cold and so
easy to catch, dreamily

moves his delicate feet
and long tail. I hold
my hand open for him to go.

Each minute the last minute.

Denise Levertov

After reading this poem, you might want to go back to an earlier one, "Beyond Time" by Mieczysław Jastrun. Both poems are concerned with the here and the now, the importance of living in the present moment if we are truly to experience our lives. And once again, a single last line set apart, not even a complete sentence, affords a little shiver of recognition and surprise.

"MAN IS BUT A CASTAWAY"

Man is but a castaway
  On this planet's shore.
He survives from day to day.
  Can he ask for more?
Vast and intricate the store
  Of his printed words.
Short and simple is the lore
  Of the beasts and birds.

Clarence Day

This short poem recalls Tomas Tranströmer's "March '79," which also contrasts the language of human beings and animals, but in another way.

HERE IN THIS SPRING

Here in this spring, stars float along the void;
Here in this ornamental winter
Down pelts the naked weather;
This summer buries a spring bird.

Symbols are selected from the years'
Slow rounding of four seasons' coasts,
In autumn teach three seasons' fires
And four birds' notes.

I should tell summer from the trees, the worms
Tell, if at all, the winter's storms
Or the funeral of the sun;
I should learn spring by the cuckooing,
And the slug should teach me destruction.

A worm tells summer better than the clock,
The slug's a living calendar of days;
What shall it tell me if a timeless insect
Says the world wears away?

Dylan Thomas

NOTHING GOLD CAN STAY

Nature's first green is gold,
Her hardest hue to hold,
Her early leaf's a flower;
But only so an hour.
Then leaf subsides to leaf.
So Eden sank to grief,
So dawn goes down to day.
Nothing gold can stay.

Robert Frost

At the heart of this lovely lyric, with its simple rhyming couplets, there is a mystery. Gold as a metallic element in nature is known for its permanence. Yet here the color gold in nature is symbolic of all that is both precious and evanescent.

GOODBYE, GOLDENEYE

Rag of black plastic, shred of a kite
caught on the telephone cable above the bay
has twisted in the wind all winter, summer, fall.

Leaves of birch and maple, brown paws of the oak
have all let go but this. Shiny black Mylar
on stem strong as fishline, the busted kite string

whipped around the wire and knotted—how long
will it cling there? Through another spring?
Long barge nudged up channel by a snorting tug,

its blunt front aproned with rot-black tires–
what is being hauled in slime-green drums?
The herring gulls that used to feed their young

on the shore—puffy, wide-beaked babies standing
spraddle-legged and crying—are not here this year.
Instead, steam shovel, bulldozer, cement mixer

rumble over sand, beginning the big new beach house.
There'll be a hotdog stand, flush toilets, trash—
Plastic and glass, greasy cartons, crushed beercans,

barrels of garbage for water rats to pick through.
So, goodbye, goldeneye, and grebe and scaup and loon.
Goodbye, morning walks beside the tide tinkling

among clean pebbles, blue mussel shells and snail
shells that look like staring eyeballs. Goodbye,
kingfisher, little green, black crowned heron,

snowy egret. And, goodbye, oh faithful pair of
swans that used to glide—god and goddess
shapes of purity—over the wide water.

May Swenson

The Common Goldeneye duck is found throughout the United States and Canada. Along with the other birds mentioned in this poem, it is losing its habitats due both to relentless construction and human carelessness. Here the Goldeneye is undoubtedly chosen to represent all its fellow birds both because of the **alliteration** of its name with "goodbye" in the title and because, as in the previous poem, "gold" symbolizes beauty and value.

THE DODO

Oh when the dodo flourished
What did the dodo do?
The dodo had such stubby wings
The dodo never flew.

Oh when the dodo had his day
What was the dodo's plan?
The dodo had such stumpy legs
The dodo never ran.

The prey of human predators,
A bird who couldn't soar,
With all his brood pursued for food
The dodo is no more.

And now, alas, the dodo's read as
Simply something to be dead as.

Isabel Wilner

"Dead as a dodo," goes the familiar phrase. An object lesson in **extinction**, the dodo was a flightless bird living on the island of Mauritius in the Indian Ocean when it was first sighted by Dutch sailors around 1600. Like the Galápagos rail, it had lost its power of flight after landing on an island with plenty of food and no predators. But when human beings arrived and cut down the forest, the dodo lost its food source. In addition, the cats, rats, and pigs brought by the sailors destroyed its nests. Eighty years later it was extinct.

SECRETARY BIRD

Take a letter:

Say that
the ancient trees are falling.
Say that
the whale's song grows faint.
Say the passenger pigeon is gone.
The great auk is gone.
The rhino, the mountain gorilla,
almost gone…

Dip your quill

in the sludge

along the river,

in the soot

from the smokestack,

in the poisoned lake,

in the burning rain.

Dip it in the blood of the great blue whale.

Take a letter, bird:

to whom it may

concern

Alice Schertle

Unlike the Dodo, the Secretary Bird is still with us, although it, too, is threatened by loss of habitat and is a protected species in Sub-Saharan Africa. A large bird of prey, mostly terrestrial, its name probably comes from its feathered crest, resembling quill-pens tucked behind the ear, once the habit of secretaries. Playing with this coincidental name, the poet dictates a somber letter.

THE GREAT AUK'S GHOST

The Great Auk's ghost rose on one leg,

Sighed thrice and three times winked

And turned and poached a phantom egg

And muttered, "I'm extinct."

Ralph Hodgson

BUFFALO DUSK

The buffalo are gone.
And those who saw the buffaloes are gone.
Those who saw the buffaloes by thousands and how they
  pawed the prairie sod into dust with their hoofs,
  their great heads down pawing on in a great pageant
  of dusk,
Those who saw the buffaloes are gone,
And the buffaloes are gone.

Carl Sandburg

As another example of species extinction, the American bison, commonly known as the buffalo, is mourned in this poem, written in 1922. Once tens of millions roamed the western plains; but by 1900 only a few remained, hunted to near-extinction by commercial interests. Then, in a remarkable turn of events, some preservation-minded ranchers captured and began to breed a few animals from the almost decimated herds. Today American bison are redistributed throughout the West on both public and private lands.

THE FLOWER-FED BUFFALOES

The flower-fed buffaloes of the spring

In the days of long ago

Ranged where the locomotives sing

And the prairie flowers lie low:

The tossing, blooming, perfumed grass

Is swept away by wheat,

Wheels and wheels and wheels spin by

In the spring that still is sweet.

But the flower-fed buffaloes of the spring

Left us long ago,

They gore no more, they bellow no more:—

With the Blackfeet lying low,

With the Pawnee lying low.

Vachel Lindsay

Carl Sandburg and Vachel Lindsay were contemporaries, born in Illinois only a year apart and both members of the Chicago School of poets. In this poem, published two years after the previous one, Lindsay, too, mourns not only the demise of the buffaloes but also the peoples who lived alongside them whose lives were so intricately intertwined with theirs.

LANDSCAPE

What will you find at the edge of the world?

A footprint,

a feather,

desert sand swirled?

A tree of ice,

a rain of stars,

or a junkyard of cars?

What will there be at the rim of the earth?

A mollusk,

a mammal,

a new creature's birth?

Eternal sunrise,

immortal sleep,

or cars piled up in a rusty heap?

Eve Merriam

WHERE WILL WE RUN TO?

Where will we run to
When the moon's
Polluted in its turn

And the sun sits
With its wheels blocked
In the used star lot?

X. J. Kennedy

EARTH'S BONDMAN

When man has conquered space
What will be his gain?
The moon's pocked face
Unmollified by rain,

The far cold reaches
Between star and star,
The blast-carved beaches
Where no seas are

Nor any wind sings
Nor any gull cries;
Where no herb springs
Nor germinates nor dies?

Though the universe be his,
The last void spanned,
Not all the galaxies
Can break his ancient bond

With cloud and leaf and sod.
The earth is in his flesh,
The tide is in his blood;
So intricate the mesh

That moors him to his star.
Adventurer by will,
By nature insular,
He wears Earth's livery still.

Betty Page Dabney

The title and the last stanza each use a somewhat unfamiliar word. A "bondman" or "bondsman" is usually an indentured servant, someone who works without wages. "Livery" is the uniform worn by such a person. Here the poet notes the impossibility of man permanently forsaking his planet, however far he may venture. The poem bids us to recognize ourselves as tied inexorably to our true home, planet Earth.

from FOUR QUARTETS

We shall not cease from exploration
And the end of all our exploring
Will be to arrive where we started
And know the place for the first time.
Through the unknown, remembered gate
When the last of earth left to discover
Is that which was the beginning;
At the source of the longest river
The voice of the hidden waterfall
And the children in the apple-tree
Not known, because not looked for
But heard, half-heard, in the stillness
Between two waves of the sea.

T. S. Eliot

WHO AM I?

The trees ask me,
And the sky,
And the sea asks me,
> *Who am I?*

The grass asks me,
And the sand,
And the rocks ask me
> *Who I am.*

The wind tells me
At nightfall,
And the rain tells me.
> *Someone small.*

Someone small
Someone small
> *But a piece*
> *of*
> *it*
> *all.*

> *Felice Holman*

MORE FUNNY IDEAS ABOUT GRANDEUR

Down House, 1844.

'To Emma, in case of my sudden death.
　　I have just finished this sketch
of my species theory. If true, as I believe,
　　it will be a considerable step
in science. My most solemn last request
　　is that you devote 400 pounds
to its publication.'

'There is grandeur, if you look
　　at every organic being
as the lineal successor of some other form,
　　now buried under thousands of feet of rock.
Or else as a co-descendant, with that buried form,
　　from some other inhabitant of this world
more ancient still, now lost.

Out of famine, death and struggle for existence,
　　comes the most exalted end
we're capable of conceiving: creation
　　of the higher animals!

Our first impulse is to disbelieve—
   how could any secondary law
produce organic beings, infinitely numerous,
characterized by most exquisite
   workmanship and adaptation?
Easier to say, a Creator designed each.
   But there is a simple grandeur in this view—
that life, with its power to grow, to reach, feel,
   reproduce, diverge, was breathed
into matter in a few forms first

and maybe only one. To say that while this planet
   has gone cycling on
according to fixed laws of gravity,
   from so simple an origin, through selection
of infinitesimal varieties, endless forms
   most beautiful and wonderful
have been, and are being, evolved.'

Ruth Padel

Shortly before this book went to press, we had a wonderful surprise. We discovered that Ruth Padel, Darwin's great-great-granddaughter, had recently published a series of poems, including this one, based on his writings. At very short notice she generously agreed to record the poem for us and offer some comments as well. "My poem," she says, "is taken from words that Darwin wrote when he was afraid that, if he died, his flash of absolute insight, that you could show how evolution worked through a process of natural selection, would not be given to the world."

THE TREE THAT TIME BUILT

Do not fret
And do not doubt.
You are in time.
You can't fall out.

No matter what
You say or do,
You are in time.
Time is in you.

And everything
That is to be
Will be in time
Upon this tree.

Mary Ann Hoberman

Glossary

ADAPTATION

In biology, the process by which a living organism adjusts to its environment.
For example, the human eye can focus both closely and on things far away as well as see in bright sunlight and in nearly total darkness. Scientists call such traits *adaptations* because they enable a group of plants or animals to reproduce successfully in their environments.

ALLITERATION

The repetition of initial identical consonant sounds or any vowel sounds in successive or closely associated words or syllables. Example: "Peter Piper picked a peck of pickled peppers."

ALTRUISM

This term has a special meaning in modern biology: it refers to individuals that seem to behave unselfishly, particularly within their own species, but also sometimes across species, at the risk of injury to themselves or even death. Some examples: food sharing; adoption of orphans; fighting without killing or even injuring an adversary. Such behavior appears to contradict the theory of natural selection, which favors the fittest and makes no provision for helping the weak. Today, the study of altruism is a vigorous area of research in evolutionary biology.

ASSONANCE

Similar vowel sounds in stressed syllables that end with different consonant sounds. Assonance differs from rhyme in that rhyme is a similarity of both vowel and consonant. Contrast *lake/fake* (rhyme) with *lake/fate* (assonance).

CELL

The smallest independently functioning unit in the structure of an organism.

CLASS

In traditional scientific nomenclature, a comprehensive group of organisms forming a category more inclusive than an order and less inclusive than a phylum.

COEVOLUTION

The evolution of two or more interdependent species, each adapting to changes in the other. For example, the coevolution of insects and the flowers they pollinate. (Contrast with convergent evolution.)

CONCRETE VERSE

Also known as *pattern poetry* or *shaped verse*. A poem so constructed that its printed version takes a form suggesting its subject matter.

CONVERGENT EVOLUTION

The process whereby organisms, not closely related, independently acquire similar characteristics in separate and sometimes varying ecosystems. An example: similarities in structure of the wings of insects, birds, and bats have evolved independently. (Contrast with coevolution.)

DNA (DEOXYRIBONUCLEIC ACID)

A natural chemical found in all living things that controls how they develop. DNA provides a clear mechanism for copying genetic information, with tremendous implications for our understanding of heredity and variation. Modern scientists have learned to read entire genomes and study genetic variation—the raw material for Darwin's evolutionary theory—in great detail.

ECOSYSTEM

A system of relations among living organisms, their surroundings, their habits, and modes of life.

Embryology

An embryo is an animal before birth or emergence from an egg. Embryology is the science relating to the embryo and its development.

Environment

The aggregate of all the external conditions and influences affecting the life and development of an organism. Environmental change is a major factor in the process of evolution.

Evolution

In its Darwinian sense, evolution refers to the tendency of species to change over generations as they adapt to their environment. A way of looking at the world that has great predictive and explanatory power, the theory of evolution has broadened and changed in the twentieth and twenty-first centuries as Darwin's theories have been integrated with genetic studies.

Extinction

The death of every member of a species.

Family

Another unit in the biological system of classification, family is less inclusive than class but more inclusive than genus.

Fossil

The word fossil comes from a Latin word meaning "to dig." A fossil is either a preserved part (bones, teeth, shells) or an impression (leaf prints, footprints) of an animal or plant that died long ago. Fossils are given Latin or Greek names usually referring to the appearance of an organism, the place where it was found, or the person who found it. This practice enables scientists to communicate with each other about fossil finds even though they may speak different languages.

Found Poem

A poem created from prose found in a non-poetic context. The lines are rearranged into a form patterned on the rhythm and appearance of poetry.

Galápagos

The Galápagos Islands lie in the Pacific Ocean, 600 miles west of Ecuador. They consist of thirteen major islands and six smaller islands. The word *Galápagos* means "tortoises" in Spanish. Many species on these islands live nowhere else on earth.

Gene

The basic unit of heredity in a living organism.

Genetics

The study of the inheritance of features that are transmitted from parents to offspring through microscopic particles called genes.

Genome

The term genome refers to the DNA from a single organism.

Genus

(plural: **genera**) A rank in taxonomy used in the classification of living and fossil organisms. Every animal and plant species has two parts to its scientific name: genus and species. The first part, genus, refers to a group of several similar species. The second part, species, refers to a particular type of animal in the group. For example, big cats belong to the genus *panthera*. Within this genus, a tiger is classified as a *panthera tigris* and a lion is a *panthera leo*.

Geology

The study of the history and structure of the earth.

Heredity

In the biological definition: the transference of biological characteristics from parent to offspring through their genes.

Hypothesis

A tentative explanation for a phenomenon used as a basis for further investigation.

Irony

A form of speech in which one meaning is stated and a different, usually opposite, meaning is intended.

Metamorphosis

A form of development from egg to adult in which there is a series of distinct stages, as in the transformation from tadpole to frog.

Metaphor

The basic figure of speech in poetry, in which one thing is described in terms of another by way of suggesting a likeness between them.

Meter

The recurrence in poetry of a rhythmic pattern.

Mutations

Mutations are small changes in DNA, occurring at random. The mechanism upon which natural selection acts, creating variation in the gene pool and providing the advantageous new traits that survive and multiply or the disadvantageous traits that die out with weaker organisms. Mutations can also be caused by exposure to ultraviolet or nuclear radiation as well as pollution. Most are harmless; many are fatal; a few may be advantageous and eventually, by means of heredity, spread throughout an entire population.

Natural History

The study and description of the whole natural world, including plants, animals, minerals, and fossils.

Natural Selection

The process in nature by which, according to Darwin's theory of evolution, only the organisms best adapted to their environment tend to survive and transmit their genetic characteristics in increasing numbers to succeeding generations, while those less adapted tend to be eliminated.

Organism

The material structure of an individual animal or plant, i.e., the organization or constitution of a living being.

Paleontology

The study of extinct forms of life through examination of their fossils.

Phylum

A division of animals or plants related by descent from a common ancestor. A phylum is part of the universal system developed by the Swedish biologist, Linnaeus, in the early eighteenth century to name and classify organisms. He grouped them by their physical characteristics, a system that became the basis for scientific classification or taxonomy.

Poetic License

A freedom allowed the poet to depart in subject matter, grammar, or diction from what would be proper in ordinary prose discourse. In a broad sense, poets are using poetic license when they invent fictions or embellish facts.

Science

From the Latin *scientia*, meaning "knowledge." The study of the physical world and its manifestations, especially by using systematic observation and experiment. Using controlled methods, scientists collect and analyze information. They develop and test hypotheses and build theories in order to understand and explain how the world works.

Sexual Selection

Darwin introduced the term "sexual selection" to refer to how members of a species compete for opportunities to breed. Both natural selection and sexual selection drive evolutionary change.

Shape Poetry

See: Concrete verse.

Species

A category in the classification of life forms. Scientists identify a species in two ways: first, all members of the same species share similar characteristics; and, second, individuals of the same species can mate with one another and produce offspring. For example, all dogs, whatever their breed, belong to the same species because they can mate with each other and have puppies which, in turn, can produce offspring. In contrast, while a horse and a mule have common characteristics and can mate, their offspring, a donkey, will not be able to reproduce. The origin of new species is an area of research that continues to be central to evolutionary studies today.

Stanza

A recurrent grouping of two or more lines of a poem in terms of length, metrical form, and rhyme scheme.

Subspecies

Populations within a species that show recognizable inherited differences from one another, but are capable of interbreeding freely.

"Survival of the fittest"

First used by Herbert Spencer in his *Principles of Biology*, this phrase was also used by Darwin as a metaphor for natural selection. It refers to the process by which only the organisms best adapted to their environment tend to survive and transmit their genetic characteristics in increasing numbers to succeeding generations, while those less adapted tend to be eliminated.

Taxonomy

The science of classifying animals and plants into different categories. The modern system is named the Linnaean taxonomic system after the Swedish biologist Carolius Linnaeus (1707–1778). It places organisms in seven major divisions, called *taxa*, as follows: Kingdom, Phylum, Class, Order, Family, Genus, Species. (You can use the following memory device or *mnemonic* as a way of remembering these divisions in order: King Phillip Came Over For Great Spaghetti. Or you can make up your own!)

Theory

In its scientific definition: an explanation based on observation, experimentation, and reasoning, especially one that has been tested and confirmed as a general principle helping to explain and predict natural phenomena.

Variation

In biology, any difference between cells, individual organisms, or groups of organisms within a species. Variation may be observed in physical appearance, fertility, mode of reproductive behavior, and other measurable characteristics. Many years after Darwin first wrote about the role of variation in natural selection, scientists discovered that variations occur through a process called mutation.

Suggestions for Further Reading and Research

Books:

Darwin, Charles. *The Autobiography of Charles Darwin, 1809–1882*. Edited by Nora Barlow. New York: W.W. Norton, 2005.

———. *The Origin of Species*, Bantam Classics, 1999.

———. *The Voyage of the Beagle*, Penguin, 1989.

Donald, Diana and Jane Munro. *Endless Forms: Charles Darwin, Natural Science, and the Visual Arts*. New Haven, CT: Yale University Press, 2009.

Eldridge, Niles. *Darwin: Discovering the Tree of Life*. New York: W.W. Norton, 2005.

Gamlin, Linda. *Evolution*. Eyewitness Books. New York: Dorling Kindersley, 2009.

Heiligman, Deborah. *Charles and Emma: The Darwins' Leap of Faith*. New York: Henry Holt, 2009.

Jenkins, Steve. *Life on Earth: The Story of Evolution*. New York: Houghton Mifflin, 2002.

Lasky, Kathryn. *John Muir: America's First Environmentalist*. Cambridge, MA: Candlewick, 2006.

Lawson, Kristan. *Darwin and Evolution for Kids*. Chicago: Chicago Review Press, 2003.

Leslie, Claire Walker and Charles E. Roth. *Keeping a Nature Journal*. North Adams, MA: Storey Publishing, 2000.

Padel, Ruth. *Darwin: A Life in Poems*. New York: Knopf, 2009.

Sheehan, Katherine and Mary Waidner. *Earth Child: Games, Stories, Activities, Experiments & Ideas about Living Lightly on Planet Earth*. Tulsa: Council Oak Books, 1992.

Sis, Peter. *The Tree of Life*: *A Book Depicting the Life of Charles Darwin*. New York: Farrar Straus Giroux, 2003.

Stein, Sara. *The Evolution Book*. New York: Workman Publishing, 1986.

Weiner, Jonathan. *The Beak of the Finch*. New York: Knopf, 1994.

Websites:

www.charliesplayhouse.com/Bibiliography.pdf—Children's Books about Evolution and Charles Darwin: An Annotated Bibliography.

www.darwinproject.ac.uk—The Darwin Correspondence Project.

http://darwin-online.org.uk—The Complete Works of Charles Darwin Online.

www.ecoliteracy.org—Center for Ecoliteracy. Dedicated to education for sustainable living (K–12).

About the Poets

VIRGINIA HAMILTON ADAIR, 1913–2004

Adair grew up in New Jersey where her earliest memories were of hearing poetry read aloud. While a student at Mt. Holyoke College, she won several poetry prizes. After her marriage, she moved to California. Although she wrote almost daily and her poems appeared in many magazines, her first book of poetry, *Ants on the Melon*, was not published until she was 83 years old.

DOROTHY ALDIS, 1896–1966

One of the most popular children's poets, Aldis was born in Chicago and published her first book in 1927. During her lifetime, she produced twenty-nine books, including biography and young adult literature as well as poetry. Her collection, *All Together* (1952), brings together many of her lively, optimistic poems.

A. R. AMMONS, 1926–2001

Raised in rural North Carolina, Ammons was the principal of an elementary school and worked in a glass company before starting to write poetry during World War II. After publishing his first book of poems at his own expense, he went on to win many major literary awards and to teach at Cornell University. His poems meticulously explore the natural world. *The Really Short Poems of A.R. Ammons* (1991) is a good introduction to his work.

HANS CHRISTIAN ANDERSEN, 1805–1875

Born in Denmark to a shoemaker and a washerwoman, Andersen left home at an early age and went to Copenhagen where a wealthy patron arranged for his formal education at a private school. He wrote plays, poems, travel books, and stories; but he is most famous for his fairy tales, including "The Princess and the Pea," "The Emperor's New Clothes," and the autobiographical "The Ugly Duckling."

WENDELL BERRY, 1934–

Berry describes himself as a farmer, essayist, conservationist, novelist, teacher, and poet. Born in Newcastle, Kentucky, he continues to farm the land his family has worked for two centuries along the Kentucky River. A committed environmentalist, he has written more than thirty books of poetry, essays, and novels. *The Gift of Gravity: Selected Poems, 1968–2000* came out in 2002.

WILLIAM BLAKE, 1757–1827

Son of a prosperous London haberdasher, Blake was apprenticed to an engraver and later studied at the Royal Academy of Art. One of the greatest English poets, he is unique in that his graphic work is integral to his writing: he etched, made watercolors, and bound most of his own books. In *Songs of Innocence* and *Songs of Experience*, he presents the world in a simple and direct manner, often from a child's point of view.

JOSEPH BRUCHAC, 1942–

Bruchac still lives in the same house in which he grew up, in the Adirondack mountain foothills of New York. He writes and tells traditional stories of Northeast Woodland Indians, drawn in part from his own Abenaki heritage. With more than seventy books for adults and children to his credit, he has also received many honors for his efforts to preserve traditional Native American skills and culture. *Bowman's Store: A Journey to Myself* (1997) is his autobiography.

ELIZABETH COATSWORTH, 1893–1986

Born in Buffalo, New York, Coatsworth spent her childhood traveling the world, crossing the deserts of Egypt on a donkey when she was five years old. During her lifetime she wrote over ninety books for children, including both poetry and novels. *The Cat Who Went to Heaven* (1930) won the 1931 Newbery Award for the best children's book. Her husband was the author and naturalist, Henry Beston.

Robert P. Tristram Coffin, 1892–1955

Coffin was raised on a salt-water farm in Brunswick, Maine. After graduating from Bowdoin College, where he later taught, he attended Oxford University as a Rhodes Scholar. In his poems and essays he often wrote about his home state and his country in a clear, sometimes colloquial, style. His book *Strange Holiness* won the Pulitzer Prize for Poetry in 1936.

Betty Page Dabney, 1911–

Betty Page Dabney was born in Norfolk, Virginia, in 1911. She received her MA from the University of Virginia and taught high school English in her hometown.

Clarence Day, 1874–1935

Born in New York City, Day was an ardent proponent of women's suffrage. He published seven books, all remarkable for his highly individual humor. *Life with Father* and, posthumously, *Life with Mother*, became American classics and provided the material for long-running plays that were also made into films.

Emily Dickinson, 1830–1886

Dickinson grew up in a prosperous and prominent family in Amherst, Massachusetts. After a short time at Mount Holyoke Female Seminary (later Mount Holyoke College), she returned home and withdrew into a life of seclusion. Although she published a few poems during her lifetime, it was not until a cache of almost 2000 poems was discovered after her death that the extent of her original and unique talent became known. She is now considered one of the great American poets.

John Drinkwater, 1882–1937

A versatile English man of letters, Drinkwater wrote historical plays, literary criticism, and autobiography, as well as several volumes of poetry. He founded a repertory theater where he worked for many years as actor, director, and general manager. He was one of the self-styled Georgian poets, who specialized in rustic verse about nature and rural life.

T. S. Eliot, 1888–1965

American-English poet, playwright, editor, and critic, Eliot was born in St. Louis, Missouri; he became a British subject in 1927. As a young man, he taught school and later worked in a bank as well as in publishing. In 1948, he won the Nobel Prize in Literature. His most famous poem, "The Waste Land," is a touchstone of modern literature.

Ralph Waldo Emerson, 1803–1882

Essayist, philosopher, poet, lecturer, and a founder of the Transcendentalist movement, Emerson was one of the most influential literary figures of the nineteenth century. Born in Boston, Massachusetts, he is perhaps most famous for his popular essays, such as "Nature" and "Self Reliance," often first given as lectures to New England audiences.

Barbara Juster Esbensen, 1925–1996

Born in Madison, Wisconsin, Esbensen knew from childhood that she wanted to be a writer. The biggest influence on her development as a writer was her high school English teacher. Esbensen published over twenty children's books, both poetry and prose, many of them dealing with nature, science, and Native American legends. *Echoes for the Eye: Poems to Celebrate Patterns in Nature* (1996) explores the interconnectedness of science, nature, and art. In 1994 she received the NCTE award for Excellence in Poetry for Children.

Rachel Field, 1894–1942

Field was born in New York City to a prominent New England family whose members included well-known doctors, judges, and engineers. Although she did not learn to read well until after she was ten years old, she managed to excel in theater by memorizing her lines as someone read them to her. She wrote fiction for adults and also plays, fiction, and poems for children. Her novel, *Hitty, Her First Hundred Years* (1929), won the Newbery Medal.

Margaret Fishback, 1900–1985

Fishback had dual careers in writing and advertising. As an author of light verse, she published many books, including *A Child's Natural History*, and her limericks and poems appeared in numerous popular magazines. In a 1932 newspaper article, she was described as "the highest-paid advertising woman in the world."

Aileen Fisher, 1906–2002

Born in Iron River, Missouri, Fisher wrote poems, fiction, and plays for children. Her love of plants and animals is evident in her poetry, which speaks of the beauty and wonder of nature. "My first and chief love," she said, "is writing children's verse. If I write something I like, children are pretty apt to like it, too. I guess what it amounts to is that I never grew up." *Sing of the Earth and Sky: Poems about Our Planets and the Wonders Beyond* was published in 2001. The NCTE award for Excellence in Poetry for Children was given to her in 1978.

Douglas Florian, 1950–

Both author and artist, Florian has written and illustrated over thirty children's books that are recognized for their wit, wordplay, and lyrical qualities. He has received many awards, including an ALA Notable Children's Book Award for *The Beast Feast*. Florian studied art at Queens College and the School of Visual Arts in New York City where he has spent most of his life and where he now lives with his wife and five children.

Robert Francis, 1901–1987

Francis, born in Upland, Pennsylvania, cultivated the art of living frugally. His poetry celebrates the virtues represented by nature, sometimes seeing natural objects as metaphors for conduct. He grew his own vegetables, herbs, and fruits on his farm in Amherst, Massachusetts, where, in addition to poems, he wrote essays and a novel. His *Collected Poems: 1936–1976* was published in 1976.

ROBERT FROST, 1874–1963

A leading American poet, Frost was born in San Francisco, California. After his father died, the ten-year-old Frost moved to his grandfather's home in Massachusetts. His best-known poems celebrate the people and the countryside of New England. He received many honors and awards, including (several times) the Pulitzer Prize for Poetry. In 1961 he recited his poem, "The Gift Outright," at President John F. Kennedy's inauguration.

ISABELLA GARDNER, 1915–1981

Born into a prominent Boston family, Gardner was named after her aunt, the art collector Isabella Stewart Gardner, founder of the museum that bears her name. Gardner first pursued an acting career but, after moving to Chicago, turned to poetry and in 1951 joined the staff of *Poetry* magazine as an editor. Her collection *That Was Then* (1979) was nominated for an American Book Award.

KRISTINE O'CONNELL GEORGE, 1954–

Author of several well-received collections of poetry for young people, George has won numerous awards, including the Myra Cohn Livingston Award for Excellence in Children's Poetry in 1999 and the Bank Street College Claudia Lewis Poetry Award in 2002. Many of her poems reflect her love of the natural world.

THOMAS HARDY, 1840–1928

One of the great nineteenth-century writers, Hardy was an English novelist and poet who inherited his love of music and literature from his parents. Apprenticed to a church architect, he continued his studies of classic Latin and Greek literature. He did not begin to write poetry until he was fifty-eight. A major theme of his unadorned, unromantic poetry is the human struggle against cosmic forces.

FLORENCE PARRY HEIDE, 1919–

Heide grew up in Pittsburgh, graduated from UCLA, worked for several years in advertising, then married and moved to Wisconsin where she raised five children. Once her children were in school, she began collaborating with a friend on songbooks, picture books, and mysteries. She wrote in many different styles and genres, from humorous to serious and picture books to young adult novels. Her most critically acclaimed work is her novel, *The Shrinking of Treehorn* (1971).

MARY ANN HOBERMAN, 1930–

Hoberman, co-editor of this anthology, was born and grew up in Stamford, Connecticut, and has lived in Connecticut most of her life. She published her first book of poems for children in 1957. Some of her most popular books are National Book Award winner *A House is a House for Me* (1978), *The Llama Who Had No Pajama* (1998), and the You Read to Me/I'll Read to You series. In 2003 she received the NCTE award for Excellence in Poetry for Children and in 2008 she was named the second United States Children's Poet Laureate by the Poetry Foundation.

RALPH HODGSON, 1871–1962

One of the English Georgian poets, Hodgson taught in Japan and later emigrated to the United States. Recognized as an outstanding translator of Japanese poetry, he also published seven volumes of his own verse on a variety of nature topics. His work was acclaimed for its simple, lyrical style. His *Collected Poems* appeared in 1961.

FELICE HOLMAN, 1919–

Born in New York City, Holman began writing poetry at an early age; her first poems were published in anthologies while she was still a student at Syracuse University. She wrote advertising copy for several years but after the birth of her daughter, she began to work as a freelance writer. Her poetry for children is included in: *At the Top of My Voice and Other Poems* (1970); *Hear You Smiling and Other Poems* (1973); and *The Song in My Head* (1985).

PATRICIA HUBBELL, 1928–

Hubbell has been writing poetry since she was eleven years old. She lives with her husband in Easton, Connecticut, the town where she was born. As a young child, she wanted to be a farmer; in college, she began studying agriculture but ultimately studied English literature instead. She has written many children's books, including ten books of poetry, among them *Earthmates* (2000) and *Black Earth, Gold Sun* (2001).

LANGSTON HUGHES, 1902–1967

Best known for his poetry, Hughes also wrote fiction, drama, autobiography, and informational books. Born in Joplin, Missouri, he grew up in Kansas, Illinois, and Ohio. As a child, he began to read as an escape from loneliness. In eighth grade, his classmates elected him Class Poet. His first poems appeared in print in his sophomore year at Central High School in Cleveland. Inspired by urban African American life, he expressed its essence in language that evoked the rhythm of jazz and blues music. The poems in his *Selected Poems* (1959) were chosen by Hughes himself and cover his entire career.

MIECZYSŁAW JASTRUN, 1903–1983

Poet, novelist, and translator, Jastrun belonged to a group of Polish writers who resisted the totalitarian regime under which he lived. He published a dozen volumes of poetry between the two world wars. Over his lifetime his work moved from political to philosophical themes; it is notable for its symbolism and elegiac tone.

TONY JOHNSTON, 1942–

After growing up in San Marino, California, and earning degrees from Stanford University, Johnston taught elementary school and worked as secretary to legendary book editor, Ursula Nordstrom. She later studied poetry writing for children with Myra Cohn Livingston. She has published over one hundred award-winning books for young readers. While living in Mexico City with her family, Johnston also wrote several books in Spanish. *An Old Shell: Poems of the Galápagos* (1999) celebrates the islands and their inhabitants.

BOBBI KATZ, 1933–

Born in Newburgh, New York, Katz is a long-time children's book editor and poet whose work has been widely anthologized. Trained as an art historian specializing in rare books, she has worked at a variety of occupations, including social worker, fashion editor, and radio show host. As an environmental activist she has also been involved with many community service projects like "weed-ins" and the Hudson River Sloop Festival. Among her many books are *Pocket Poems* (2004) and *Trailblazers: Poems of Exploration* (2007).

X. J. KENNEDY, 1929–

Poet, translator, editor, and anthologist, Kennedy was born in Dover, New Jersey. As a writer of both light and serious verse, he has received numerous awards and honors, including the 2000 NCTE award for Excellence in Poetry for Children. *Talking Like the Rain: A Read-to-Me Book of Poems* (1992), co-edited with his wife Dorothy M. Kennedy, remains one of the best poetry anthologies for young people. He has described himself as "one of an endangered species: people who still write in meter and rime."

GALWAY KINNELL, 1927–

Born in Providence, Rhode Island, Kinnell responded at a young age to the poetry of Emily Dickinson and Edgar Allen Poe. After graduating from Princeton, he traveled throughout Europe and the Middle East, returning home to work with CORE (Congress of Racial Equality) during the civil rights era of the 1960s. Later, he taught at New York University. His many books of poetry include his *Selected Poems* (1982), which won both the Pulitzer Prize and the National Book Award.

MAXINE KUMIN, 1925–

Kumin was born in Philadelphia, Pennsylvania. After teaching at Tufts and various other colleges, she moved to a farm in New Hampshire where she and her husband have bred Arabian and quarter horses. She has written both children's and adult poetry and received the Pulitzer Prize for Poetry in 1973 for *Up Country*. From 1981–82 she served at the Poet Laureate poetry consultant to the Library of Congress.

D. H. LAWRENCE, 1885–1930

One of England's leading writers, Lawrence was raised in the coal mining town of Eastwood in Nottinghamshire, England, which provided a setting for much of his fiction. After receiving a teaching certificate, he taught school for a few years, but with the publication of his first novel he became a full-time author. Later in his life he traveled to the United States and settled for a time in Taos, New Mexico. Although best-known for his novels, he wrote over eight hundred poems, including those about nature collected in *Birds, Beasts, and Flowers* (1923).

DENISE LEVERTOV, 1923–1997

Levertov was born and educated in England and emigrated to the United States in 1948. Poet, essayist, translator, and political activist, she writes in a spare and deceptively simple way both about issues of concern to women and about the human condition in modern-day life. Her first American collection of poems was *Here and Now* (1957).

CONSTANCE LEVY, 1931–

An award-winning children's poet, Levy was born and raised in St. Louis, Missouri. As a child she describes herself as observant and nature-oriented. While working as an elementary school teacher, she began to write children's books, including her first book of poetry, *I'm Going to Pet a Worm Today* (1991).

VACHEL LINDSAY, 1879–1931

Born in Springfield, Illinois, Lindsay was influenced by growing up in a town associated with American history and with Abraham Lincoln, its most famous resident. He studied both art and poetry and later became a modern-day troubadour, going on walking tours to sell his poems and drawings. His work has a quality of spoken music, often including jazz rhythms. *Rhymes to Be Traded for Bread* (1912) and *The Chinese Nightingale and Other Poems* (1917) are among his best-known volumes of poetry.

MYRA COHN LIVINGSTON, 1926–1996

Children's poet, musician, critic, educator, and anthologist, Livingston was born in Omaha, Nebraska. During her lifetime she published more than fifty volumes of poems. As a mentor to many aspiring poets, she had enormous influence in the field of children's poetry. Her collections include *Sky Songs* (1984) and *Festivals* (1996). Among her many honors was the 1980 NCTE award for Excellence in Poetry for Children.

DAVID McCORD, 1897–1997

As a children's poet, McCord wrote verse ranging from the nonsense chanting of "Pickety Fence" to the universal wondering of "Take Sky." He was born in New York and spent his childhood in New Jersey and Oregon. Among his more than fifty books are *Far and Few: Rhymes of the Never Was and Always Is* (1952) and his collected poems, *One at a Time* (1978). In 1956 he received Harvard University's first honorary Doctorate of Humane Letters and in 1977 the NCTE award for Excellence in Poetry for Children.

EVE MERRIAM, 1896–1992

Author, poet, and playwright, Merriam was born in Philadelphia, Pennsylvania, and began writing poems when she was seven. She wrote poetry and plays for adults as well as many books of poetry for children, including *It Doesn't Always Have to Rhyme* (1964) and *The Inner City Mother Goose* (1971), which became a Broadway musical. In 1981, she won the NCTE award for Excellence in Poetry for Children.

W. S. MERWIN, 1927–

Over a long career, Merwin has expressed his devotion to our planet in both poems and essays. Born in New York City, he grew up in New Jersey and Pennsylvania. Among numerous awards, in 1971, he won the Pulitzer Prize for Poetry; and he has served as Consultant in Poetry to the Library of Congress. His latest book, *The Shadow of Sirius*, published in 2009, won another Pulitzer Prize. He now lives in Hawaii where he is involved with the restoration of rainforests.

LILIAN MOORE, 1909–2004

Editor, educator, and poet, Moore pioneered the program that made quality paperback books affordable for elementary school children throughout the United States. She was born in New York City to immigrant parents, attended city schools, and later became a reading specialist. Among her many poetry collections are *I Thought I Heard the City* (1969) and *Poems Have Roots* (1997), which records her observations of nature.

CHRISTIAN MORGENSTERN, 1871–1914

A German essayist, translator, and poet, Morgenstern found inspiration for much of his poetry in English literary nonsense. Among the English translations of his work is *Lullabies, Lyrics and Gallows Songs* (1995). His humorous poems often have a subtle, profoundly serious streak.

Jeff Moss, 1942–1998

Moss was a founding writer and composer-lyricist on *The Muppet Show*. Born in New York City, he won fifteen Emmys for his work as well as several awards for his recordings and an Academy Award nomination. *The Butterfly Jar* (1989), *On the Other Side of the Door* (1991), and *Bones* (1997) are his poetry collections for children.

Ogden Nash, 1902–1971

Elected to the National Institute of Arts and Letters in 1950, Nash was a keen observer of American life. He was born in Rye, New York. His satiric and humorous verse poked fun at human foibles. While the fact that he specialized in light verse prevented him from being considered as a "serious" poet, he continues to be one of the most widely read and quoted poets ever published. He also wrote plays and published two collections of poetry for children: *The Boy Who Laughed at Santa Claus* (1957) and *Girls Are Silly* (1962).

Mary Oliver, 1935–

Oliver's work reflects her communion with the natural world, first inspired by her rural Ohio upbringing and later by her adopted home of New England. She has received numerous awards and honors, including the Pulitzer Prize for *American Primitive* (1983) and the National Book Award for *New and Selected Poems* (1992). In 1999 and 2000, her book-length poem, *The Leaf and the Cloud*, was included in *Best American Poetry of the Year*.

Ruth Padel, 1946–

Classicist, poet, and journalist, Padel was born in London. Along with her poetry, she has written an acclaimed nature book, *Tigers in Red Weather*. *Darwin: A Life in Poems* (2009) chronicles the life of her great-great-grandfather, Charles Darwin.

LISA WESTBERG PETERS, 1951–

Mountain climber, bird watcher, and fossil finder, Peters has written books, novels, and verse for a young audience. Born in Minneapolis, Minnesota, she grew up in St. Paul where she now lives. Among her titles are *Our Family Tree: An Evolution Story* (2003) and *Earthshake: Poems from the Ground Up* (2003).

SYLVIA PLATH, 1932–1963

Plath was born in Jamaica Plain, Massachusetts, and published her first poem in the *Boston Sunday Herald* when she was eight years old. She later attended Smith College and went on to win many academic and literary awards. Her first collection of poems was *Colossus* (1960). In addition to her poetry, she wrote *The Bell Jar* (1963), an autobiographical novel.

JACK PRELUTSKY, 1940–

In 2006, Prelutsky was named the first United States Children's Poet Laureate by the Poetry Foundation and has won numerous other awards and honors. Born in Brooklyn, New York, he has published more than thirty volumes of original verse and anthologies of children's poetry, including *Behold the Bold Umbrellaphant and Other Poems* (2006) and *The Beauty and the Beast: Poems from the Animal Kingdom* (2006).

KATHLEEN RAINE, 1908–2003

English poet and critic, Raine published her first book of poems, *Stone and Flower*, in 1943 and her last, *The Collected Poems of Kathleen Raine*, in 2000. Her poems and essays assert that true poetry is an expression of the spirit, indicating a reality often hidden by the outward appearance of things. In 1992, she was awarded the Queen's Medal for Poetry.

E. V. RIEU, 1887–1972

A celebrated translator from Latin and Greek, English poet Emile Victor Rieu founded the Penguin Classics where he published his translation of Homer's *Odyssey* in 1946. His books of children's verse include *Cuckoo Calling: a Book of Verse for Youthful People* (1933) and *The Flattered Flying Fish and Other Poems* (1962).

Rainer Maria Rilke, 1875–1926

Born in Prague, Rilke lived in Germany, France, and Switzerland. Widely regarded as a master of modern verse, his topics range from the simple to the elaborate and profound. Among his best-known works are *The Book of Hours* (1906), *Duino Elegies* (1923), and *Sonnets to Orpheus* (1923). His work has been translated into English by many well-known poets.

Theodore Roethke, 1908–1963

As a boy growing up in Saginaw, Michigan, Roethke spent much of his time in his father's greenhouse. What he learned and observed there greatly influenced his poetry, as did the poets Dylan Thomas and Walt Whitman. Many of his poems are concerned with the natural world and the human being's place within it. His collection, *The Waking* (1954), won the Pulitzer Prize.

Christina Rossetti, 1830–1894

Born into an artistic family in London, Rossetti's appreciation of nature began as she roamed the grounds of her grandparents' house in the countryside thirty miles from the city. The sister of Dante Gabriel Rossetti, the Pre-Raphaelite poet, she wrote ballads, lyrics on spiritual topics, and a collection of verses for children, *Sing-Song* (1872). Her best-known work is *Goblin Market and Other Poems* (1862).

Jelaluddin Rumi, 1207–1273

Islamic Persian sage and poet mystic, Rumi's major work is contained in six volumes of spiritual teaching and Sufi lore in the form of stories and lyric poetry.

Carl Sandburg, 1878–1967

Sandburg was born in Galesburg, Illinois, into a family of Swedish immigrants where English was a second language. He won the Pulitzer Prize twice, once for his poetry and again for his biography of Abraham Lincoln. His *Rootabaga Stories* (1920) for children were prompted by his wish to write "American fairy tales" for American children. His *Poems for Children Nowhere Near Old Enough to Vote* (1999) was compiled after his death.

Alice Schertle, 1941–

With over two dozen picture books to her credit, many in verse, Schertle (rhymes with "turtle") published *We*, a picture book of poems on the topic of evolution, in 2007. She was born in Los Angeles, attended the University of Southern California, and later taught elementary school. She now lives in Massachusetts. Her award-winning books include *Advice for a Frog and Other Poems* (1995) about unusual and endangered animals.

Karen I. Shragg, 1954–

Manager/naturalist of Wood Lake Nature Center in Richfield, Minnesota, Shragg is the author of several books for children and co-editor of *Tree Stories* (2002) where her poem "Think Like A Tree" first appeared.

Joyce Sidman, 1956–

Born in Hartford, Connecticut, Sidman now lives in Minnesota. A teacher as well as a writer, she has published many books of poetry for children, including *Butterfly Eyes and Other Secrets of the Meadow* (2006) and *Red Sings from Treetops: A Year in Color* (2009).

Marilyn Singer, 1948–

An award-winning author of more than seventy books in many genres for children and young adults, Singer was born in New York City and started out as a high school English teacher. Her parallel poetry collections, *Turtle in July* (1989) and *Fireflies at Midnight* (2003), both have nature as their major theme.

Ikkyu Sojun, 1394–1481

Poet, calligrapher, and musician, Sojun was an eccentric Japanese Zen Buddhist priest and poet. His poetry captures the immediacy, insight, and lack of pretense of Zen practice.

May Swenson, 1913–1989

Born in Logan, Utah, Swenson, was particularly interested in nature and scientific research as a poet. The recipient of many awards and honors, she published ten books of poetry, including three collections of poems for younger readers: *Poems to Solve* (1966), *More Poems to Solve* (1968), and *Iconographs* (1970).

Wisława Szymborska, 1923–

A Polish poet, Szymborska was largely unknown in the West until she won the Nobel Prize for Literature in 1996. Her poems have been translated into many languages, including English. *Poems New and Collected* (2000), translated by Stanislaw Baranczak and Clare Cavanagh, won the PEN Translation Prize.

Dylan Thomas, 1914–1953

Thomas's early infatuation with the sound of nursery rhymes influenced his highly rhythmic and musical poetry. Born in Wales, his recordings and reading tours throughout the United States popularized poetry reading as a new medium for the art. His many books, both poetry and prose, include his *Collected Poems* (1952) and *A Child's Christmas in Wales* (1955).

Tomas Tranströmer, 1931–

One of Sweden's most important poets, Tranströmer's work has been translated into more than fifty languages. He has read his nature poetry and his more intimate personal poems to audiences at many American universities. His books of poetry include the *Great Enigma: New Collected Poems* (2003).

MARK VAN DOREN, 1984–1973

Poet, novelist, and critic, Van Doren was born in Hope, Illinois, and raised on his family's farm. He taught at Columbia University for four decades and the annual Mark Van Doren Award, honoring a great teacher, was later established in his honor. In 1946 his *Collected Poems* won the Pulitzer Prize.

DAVID WAGONER, 1926–

Born in Massillon, Ohio, Wagoner has written criticism, short stories, ten novels, and twenty-three volumes of poetry. He has said that his move from the Midwest to the Pacific Northwest changed his consciousness; his poems deal with the natural environment of his adopted environment. The recipient of many awards, his *Collected Poems* (1977) and *In Broken Country* (1979) were both nominated for National Book Awards.

WALT WHITMAN, 1819–1892

Often considered the greatest American poet, Whitman celebrates the freedom and dignity of the individual, praises democracy, and extols the brotherhood of man. Born on Long Island, he volunteered as a nurse during the Civil War. His self-published *Leaves of Grass*, appearing in 1855, may be the most influential volume of poetry in the history of American literature.

ISABEL WILNER, 1920–

Born in Shanghai, China, the daughter of Episcopal missionaries, Wilner returned to the United States to attend college. She was a children's librarian for many years, during which time she published *The Poetry Troupe* (1977), an anthology of children's poetry to be read aloud. Also the author of *B is for Bethlehem* (2004), she worked for many years with elementary school children, teaching them to read, write, and memorize poetry.

Valerie Worth, 1933–1994

Most widely known for her collection, *All the Small Poems* (1994), Worth was a poet of ordinary things which she wrote about in a deceptively simple way. She was born in Philadelphia, Pennsylvania, and lived for a time in Bangalore, India, where her biologist father was studying malaria. She graduated from Swarthmore College. Also a novelist, she received the 1991 NCTE Award for Excellence in Children's Poetry.

Elinor Wylie, 1885–1928

Poet and novelist, Wylie was born in Somerville, New Jersey, and raised in Washington, D.C. Both an artist and writer, she was encouraged to concentrate on her writing efforts by Edmund Wilson, the prominent literary critic, and John Dos Passos, the novelist. She had early success with her poetry collection, *Nets to Catch the Wind* (1921), and later wrote eight novels and several more volumes of poetry.

Yokoi Yayu, 1703–1783

A poet from a distinguished old family whose father was also a haikai poet, Yayu's artistic works included painting, music, and flower arranging, but he is best known for his compilation of poetry, entitled *Rags and Tatters: The Uzuragoromo of Yokoi Yayu*. He also composed some of the most graceful and appealing prose written in Japanese.

About the Illustrator

Barbara Fortin recently moved from the foothills of the Rocky Mountains in western Canada to the small narrow streets of Old Quebec City. Her professional training in Dance and Fine Arts and her enthusiasm to cross boundaries of language and culture have allowed her to work on a variety of wonderful projects. Visit her at www.bellocchioillustration.com.

About the Compilers

Mary Ann Hoberman is a poet and the critically acclaimed author of many books for children, including the beloved *A House is a House for Me*, winner of a National Book Award. Other popular titles include *The Seven Silly Eaters* and the You Read to Me, I'll Read to You series. In 2008, she was named Children's Poet Laureate of America by the Poetry Foundation.

Linda Winston, a cultural anthropologist and teacher, has worked with students of all ages, from kindergarten through graduate school. She is the author of *Keepsakes: Using Family Stories in Elementary Classrooms* and *Grandpartners: Intergenerational Learning and Civic Renewal, K–6*.

Acknowledgments

We are so grateful to everyone who has helped us bring this true labor of love to birth. Our thanks go above all to Amy O'Donnell, who set us off on the right track and gave us the book's title. Others who offered invaluable advice and support are: Sandra Berris, Deborah Heiligman, Norman Hoberman, Perry Hoberman, Diane Louie, Elaine Magliaro, Christian McEwen, Judy O'Malley, Ann Prewitt, William "Bill" Schiller, Lyle Warner, Jonathan Weiner, John Winston, Carrie Silberman, Head Librarian of the Children's Department at the New York Society Library, and all the library staff. To our agent, Gina Maccoby, our deepest thanks for her faith in this project and her instinct in guiding it toward the perfect home. And to all the folks at Sourcebooks, whose enthusiasm and skill have made the whole publication process one of joy, our heartfelt appreciation: publisher, Dominique Raccah; editorial director, Todd Stocke; project editor, Kelly Barrales-Saylor; publicity manager, Heather Moore; and marketing director, Melanie Thompson.

And with special thanks to all the poets who recorded their poems for the disk that accompanies this book.

Permissions

All efforts have been made by the editors to contact the copyright holders for the material used in this book. The editors regret any omissions that may have occurred and will correct any such errors in future editions of this book.

Virginia Hamilton Adair: "Ants on the Melon" and "Early Walk" from *Ants on the Melon* by Virginia Hamilton Adair, copyright © 1996 by Virginia Hamilton Adair. Used by permission of Random House, Inc.

Dorothy Aldis: "Every Insect" from *Quick as a Wink* by Dorothy Aldis, copyright © 1960 by Dorothy Aldis, renewed © 1988 by Roy E. Porter. Used by permission of G. P. Putnam's Sons, A Division of Penguin Young Readers Group, A Member of Penguin Group (USA) Inc., 345 Hudson Street, New York, NY 10014. All rights reserved.

A. R. Ammons: "Bees Stopped," "Dunes," and "Height" from *Collected Poems 1951–1971* by A. R. Ammons. Copyright © 1972 by A. R. Ammons. Used by permission of W. W. Norton & Company, Inc.; "Spruce Woods" from *Worldly Hopes* by A. R. Ammons,. Copyright © 1982 by A. R. Ammons. Used by permission of W. W. Norton & Company, Inc.

Wendell Berry: "For the Future" by Wendell Berry. Copyright © 1987 by Wendell Berry from *The Collected Poems of Wendell Berry, 1957–1982*. Reprinted by permission of Counterpoint.

Joseph Bruchac: "Feathers" (text and audio) by Joseph Bruchac. All rights reserved.

Elizabeth Coatsworth: "Nosegay" by Elizabeth Coatsworth. Used by permission of Paterson Marsh Ltd. on behalf of the Estate of Elizabeth Coatsworth.

Robert P. Tristam Coffin: "The Spider" by Robert P. Tristam Coffin. Reprinted with the permission of Scribner, a Division of Simon & Schuster, Inc. from *Collected Poems of Robert P. Tristam Coffin*. Copyright © 1935 The Macmillan Company; copyright renewed © 1963 Margaret Coffin Halvosa.

Clarence Day: "Man is but a Castaway" by Clarence Day. Reprinted with permission of Wilhelmine Day Blower. All rights reserved.

T. S. Eliot: Excerpt from "Little Gidding" in *Four Quartets*, copyright © 1942 by T. S. Eliot and renewed 1970 by Esme Valerie Eliot, reprinted by permission of Houghton Mifflin Harcourt Publishing Company.

Barbara Juster Esbenson: Excerpt from "Circles" by Barbara Juster Esbenson. Text copyright © 1996 by Barbara Juster Esbensen. Used by permission of HarperCollins Publishers.

Rachel Field: "Something Told the Wild Geese" by Rachel Field. Reprinted with the permission of Atheneum Books for Young Readers, an imprint of Simon & Schuster Children's Publishing Division from *Poems* by Rachel Field. Copyright © 1934 Macmillan Publishing Company; copyright renewed © 1962 Arthur S. Penderson.

Aileen Fisher: "The World Around Us" (text and audio) by Aileen Fisher. From *Sing of the Earth and Sky* by Aileen Fisher. Copyright © 2001 by Aileen Fisher. Used by permission of Marian Reiner on behalf of the Boulder Public Library Foundation, Inc.

Douglas Florian: "The Chameleon" (text and audio) from *Lizards, Frogs and Polliwogs*, copyright © 2001

from *How to Cross a Pond: Poems about Water* by Marilyn Singer, copyright © 2003 by Marilyn Singer. Used by permission of Random House Children's Books, a division of Random House, Inc.

May Swenson: "October Textures" and "Goodbye, Goldeneye" (text and audio) by May Swenson. Reprinted with permission of the Literary Estate of May Swenson.

Dylan Thomas: "Here in this Spring" by Dylan Thomas, from *The Poems of Dylan Thomas*, copyright © 1939 by New Directions Publishing Corp. Reprinted by permission of New Directions Publishing Corp.

Tomas Tranströmer: Excerpt from "March '79," translated by Robert Bly, from *The Half-Finished Heaven: The Best Poems of Tomas Tranströmer*. Translation copyright © 2001 by Robert Bly. Reprinted with the permission of Graywolf Press, Saint Paul, Minnesota, www.graywoldpress.org. Excerpt from "March '79" by Tomas Tranströmer, translated by Robin Robertson. Reprinted by permission of Enitharmon Press, all rights reserved.

David Wagoner: "Lost" by David Wagoner. From *Traveling Light: Collected and New Poems*. Copyright © 1999 by David Wagoner. Used with permission of the poet and the University of Illinois Press.

Elinor Wylie: "The Tortoise in Eternity" from *The Collected Poems of Elinor Wylie* by Elinor Wylie, copyright © 1932 by Alfred A. Knopf, a division of Random House, Inc, copyright renewed 1960 by Edwina C. Rubenstein. Used by permission of Alfred A. Knopf, a division of Random House, Inc.

Yokoi Yayu: "A discovery!" by Yayu from *Birds, Frogs, and Moonlight*, translated by Sylvia Cassedy and Kunihiro Suetake. Copyright © 1967 by Doubleday & Co. Used by permission of Ellen Cassedy.

AUDIO

Mary Ann Hoberman and Linda Winston recorded by Bob Blank at Blank Productions in Greenwich, Connecticut.

Karen I. Shragg, Lisa Westberg Peters, Robert Bly, and Joyce Sidman recorded by Todd Melby in Minneapolis, Minnesota.

Bobbi Katz recorded by Joshua Miller at Mohonk Mountain Stage Company in New Paltz, New York.

Patricia Hubbell recorded by Paul Avgerinos at Studio Unicorn in Redding, Connecticut.

Joseph Bruchac recorded by Charlie Eble at Wood's End Recording Studio in Greenfield Center, New York.

Coleman Barks recorded by Michael Cardin at WUGA in Athens, Georgia.

Ruth Padel recorded by Simon Weir at The Classical Recording Company in London, United Kingdom.

Marilyn Singer recorded by Scott Friedlander in Brooklyn, New York.

X. J. Kennedy recorded by Josh Kennedy.

Jack Prelutsky recorded by Katy Kavanaugh at Rainstorm Studio in Bellevue, Washington.

Kristine O'Connell George recorded by Judy Crescenzo, edited by Phil Crescenzo at Cinemafuture in Oak Park, California.

Alan Cheuse recorded by Sonari Glinton at NPR in Washington, DC.

Constance Levy recorded by Mary Edwards at KWMU in St. Louis, Missouri.

Alice Schertle recorded by Bart Rankin at WFCR in Amherst, Massachusetts.

Index